C-1467   CAREER EXAMINATION SERIES

This is your
PASSBOOK for...

Security Officer

Test Preparation Study Guide
Questions & Answers

COPYRIGHT NOTICE

This book is SOLELY intended for, is sold ONLY to, and its use is RESTRICTED to individual, bona fide applicants or candidates who qualify by virtue of having seriously filed applications for appropriate license, certificate, professional and/or promotional advancement, higher school matriculation, scholarship, or other legitimate requirements of education and/or governmental authorities.

This book is NOT intended for use, class instruction, tutoring, training, duplication, copying, reprinting, excerption, or adaptation, etc., by:

1) Other publishers
2) Proprietors and/or Instructors of "Coaching" and/or Preparatory Courses
3) Personnel and/or Training Divisions of commercial, industrial, and governmental organizations
4) Schools, colleges, or universities and/or their departments and staffs, including teachers and other personnel
5) Testing Agencies or Bureaus
6) Study groups which seek by the purchase of a single volume to copy and/or duplicate and/or adapt this material for use by the group as a whole without having purchased individual volumes for each of the members of the group
7) Et al.

Such persons would be in violation of appropriate Federal and State statutes.

PROVISION OF LICENSING AGREEMENTS – Recognized educational, commercial, industrial, and governmental institutions and organizations, and others legitimately engaged in educational pursuits, including training, testing, and measurement activities, may address request for a licensing agreement to the copyright owners, who will determine whether, and under what conditions, including fees and charges, the materials in this book may be used them. In other words, a licensing facility exists for the legitimate use of the material in this book on other than an individual basis. However, it is asseverated and affirmed here that the material in this book CANNOT be used without the receipt of the express permission of such a licensing agreement from the Publishers. Inquiries re licensing should be addressed to the company, attention rights and permissions department.

All rights reserved, including the right of reproduction in whole or in part, in any form or by any means, electronic or mechanical, including photocopying, recording, or by any information storage and retrieval system, without permission in writing from the Publisher.

Copyright © 2024 by
National Learning Corporation

212 Michael Drive, Syosset, NY 11791
(516) 921-8888 • www.passbooks.com
E-mail: info@passbooks.com

PUBLISHED IN THE UNITED STATES OF AMERICA

PASSBOOK® SERIES

THE *PASSBOOK® SERIES* has been created to prepare applicants and candidates for the ultimate academic battlefield – the examination room.

At some time in our lives, each and every one of us may be required to take an examination – for validation, matriculation, admission, qualification, registration, certification, or licensure.

Based on the assumption that every applicant or candidate has met the basic formal educational standards, has taken the required number of courses, and read the necessary texts, the *PASSBOOK® SERIES* furnishes the one special preparation which may assure passing with confidence, instead of failing with insecurity. Examination questions – together with answers – are furnished as the basic vehicle for study so that the mysteries of the examination and its compounding difficulties may be eliminated or diminished by a sure method.

This book is meant to help you pass your examination provided that you qualify and are serious in your objective.

The entire field is reviewed through the huge store of content information which is succinctly presented through a provocative and challenging approach – the question-and-answer method.

A climate of success is established by furnishing the correct answers at the end of each test.

You soon learn to recognize types of questions, forms of questions, and patterns of questioning. You may even begin to anticipate expected outcomes.

You perceive that many questions are repeated or adapted so that you can gain acute insights, which may enable you to score many sure points.

You learn how to confront new questions, or types of questions, and to attack them confidently and work out the correct answers.

You note objectives and emphases, and recognize pitfalls and dangers, so that you may make positive educational adjustments.

Moreover, you are kept fully informed in relation to new concepts, methods, practices, and directions in the field.

You discover that you are actually taking the examination all the time: you are preparing for the examination by "taking" an examination, not by reading extraneous and/or supererogatory textbooks.

In short, this PASSBOOK®, used directedly, should be an important factor in helping you to pass your test.

SECURITY OFFICER

Duties

As a Security Officer, you would protect occupants of buildings or offices from outside annoyances and interference by unauthorized persons. You would monitor and maintain security systems and/or conduct scheduled rounds to control access to buildings and restricted areas. You would prevent trespassing, loitering, theft and property damage, making arrests when necessary, and appearing as a witness against persons arrested. You would also assist clients by directing them to appropriate locations, or by providing non-technical information. A Security officer may inspect building fire and safety equipment, direct people to emergency egress routes and give first aid. A Security Officer may prepare and write reports involving incidents or accidents, and may perform other duties as assigned such as attend administrative hearings as directed to maintain safety and decorum. Appointees may be required to work various shifts and unscheduled overtime, when necessary.

SUBJECT OF EXAMINATION
The written test is designed to test for knowledge, skills, and/or abilities in such areas as:
1. Applying written information in a safety and security setting;
2. Following directions (maps);
3. Preparing written; and
4. Understanding and interpreting written information.

INTRODUCTION

This test guide provides a general description of the most common subject areas which will be tested and an explanation of the different types of questions you may see on the test.

Not all subject areas tested in the Safety and Security Series are covered in this test guide. The Examination Announcement will list the subject areas that will be included on the particular test you will be taking. Some of these subject areas may not be covered in this test guide.

The most common subject areas included in the Safety and Security Series are:

1. **APPLYING WRITTEN INFORMATION IN A SAFETY AND SECURITY SETTING:** These questions evaluate your ability to read, interpret and apply rules, regulations, directions, written narratives and other related material. You will be required to read a set of information and to appropriately apply the information to situations similar to those typically experienced in a public safety and security service setting. All information needed to answer the questions is contained in the rules, regulations, etc. which are cited.

2. **FOLLOWING DIRECTIONS (MAPS):** These questions test your ability to follow physical/geographic directions using street maps or building maps. You will have to read and understand a set of directions and then use them on a simple map.

3. **PREPARING WRITTEN MATERIAL:** These questions test for the ability to present information clearly and accurately, and to organize paragraphs logically and comprehensibly. For some questions, you will be given information in two or three sentences, followed by four restatements of the information. You must then choose the best version. For other questions, you will be given paragraphs with their sentences out of order. You must then choose, from among four choices, the best order for the sentences.

4. **PRINCIPLES AND PRACTICES OF SAFETY AND SECURITY:** These questions test for a knowledge of the proper principles and practices in the field of safety and security. The questions will cover such areas as selecting the best course of action to take in a safety or security related situation.

5. **SAFETY AND SECURITY METHODS AND PROCEDURES:** These questions test for knowledge of the methods and procedures utilized in safety and security related positions. The questions cover such areas as principles and practices of safety and security precautions in a building or grounds setting, accident prevention, proper response to safety or security related incidents, the investigation of incidents, and the inspection of buildings or grounds for potential safety and/or security problems.

INTRODUCTION – CONTINUED

6. **UNDERSTANDING AND INTERPRETING WRITTEN MATERIAL:** These questions test how well you comprehend written material. You will be provided with brief reading selections and will be asked questions about the selections. All the information required to answer the questions will be presented in the selections; you will not be required to have any special knowledge relating to the subject areas of the selections.

7. **SUPERVISION:** These questions test for knowledge of the principles and practices employed in planning, organizing, and controlling the activities of a work unit toward predetermined objectives. The concepts covered, usually in a situational question format, include such topics as assigning and reviewing work; evaluating performance; maintaining work standards; motivating and developing subordinates; implementing procedural change; increasing efficiency; and dealing with problems of absenteeism, morale, and discipline.

8. **ADMINISTRATIVE SUPERVISION:** These questions test for knowledge of the principles and practices involved in directing the activities of a large subordinate staff, including subordinate supervisors. Questions relate to the personal interactions between an upper level supervisor and his/her subordinate supervisors in the accomplishment of objectives. These questions cover such areas as assigning work to and coordinating the activities of several units, establishing and guiding staff development programs, evaluating the performance of subordinate supervisors, and maintaining relationships with other organizational sections.

The remainder of this test guide explains how you will be tested in each subject area listed above. A **TEST TASK** is provided for each subject area. This is an explanation of how a question is presented and how to correctly answer it. Read each explanation carefully. This test guide also provides at least one **SAMPLE QUESTION** for each subject area. The sample question is similar to the type of questions that will be presented on the actual test. This test guide provides the **SOLUTION** and correct answer to each sample question. You should study each sample question and solution in order to understand how the correct answer was determined.

At the end of this test guide we have included a **PRACTICE TEST** which includes additional examples of the types of questions you may see on your written test. Answers are provided in the Practice Test Key so that you can see how well you have done.

SUBJECT AREA 1

APPLYING WRITTEN INFORMATION IN A SAFETY AND SECURITY SETTING: These questions evaluate your ability to read, interpret and apply rules, regulations, directions, written narratives and other related material. You will be required to read a set of information and to appropriately apply the information to situations similar to those typically experienced in a public safety and security service setting. All information needed to answer the questions is contained in the rules, regulations, etc. which are cited.

TEST TASK: You will be given a set of rules, regulations, or other written information to read. You will then be asked a question which requires you to apply the rule to a given situation.

SAMPLE QUESTION:

RULE: While patrolling your grounds or building, keep a notebook and pencil with you. Keep the following emergency phone numbers in the notebook: police, fire department, nearby hospitals, alarm company, your supervisor, and the head of your building.

When you observe something out of the ordinary, take notes. Describe what is unusual, people who are unfamiliar, and any suspicious activity. If a crime or offense takes place, record what happened, who was involved, physical appearance of the suspect, clothing worn by the suspect, time and date, names and phone numbers of witnesses, where suspect was last seen, and any physical evidence found.

SITUATION: While you are doing your rounds at 11:20 p.m. you notice a door that has been left ajar. The door opens to the office of the Assistant Director of your facility. The door is typically closed and locked for the day when the Assistant Director leaves, usually between 5:00 and 6:00 p.m. The office is dark and no one is there.

QUESTION: Based solely on the above Rule and Situation, what, if anything, should be recorded in your notebook?

A. The office was dark when you entered it.
B. No one was in the office.
C. The door was open at 11:20 p.m.
D. No entry needs to be made.

The correct answer to this sample question is choice C.

SOLUTION: *The Situation states that while doing your rounds at 11:20 p.m., you notice a door left ajar. This door is typically closed and locked for the day between 5:00 and 6:00 p.m. by the Assistant Director. The question asks what, if anything, you should record about this incident in your notebook. To answer the question, evaluate all of the choices.*

Solution continued on next page.

SUBJECT AREA 1 – CONTINUED

Choice A states that you should record in your notebook the fact that the office was dark when you entered it. The Rule states that you should take notes when you observe something out of the ordinary. It is not out of the ordinary for the Assistant Director's office to be dark at 11:20 p.m. since the Assistant Director usually leaves for the day between 5:00 and 6:00 p.m. Choice A is incorrect.

Choice B states that you should record in your notebook the fact that no one was in the office. The Rule states that you should take notes when you observe something out of the ordinary. It is not out of the ordinary for the Assistant Director's office to be unoccupied at 11:20 p.m. since the Assistant Director is not usually at work after 6:00 p.m. Choice B is incorrect.

Choice C states that you should record in your notebook the fact that the door was open at 11:20 p.m. The Rule states that you should take notes when you observe something out of the ordinary. It is out of the ordinary for the Assistant Director's office door to be open at 11:20 p.m. because the door is typically closed and locked when the Assistant Director leaves for the day, usually between 5:00 and 6:00 p.m. Choice C is the correct answer.

Choice D states that you should make no entry in your notebook. The Rule states that you should take notes when you observe something out of the ordinary. It is out of the ordinary for the Assistant Director's office door to be open at 11:20 p.m. because the door is typically closed and locked when the Assistant Director leaves for the day, usually between 5:00 and 6:00 p.m. Choice D is incorrect.

SUBJECT AREA 2

FOLLOWING DIRECTIONS (MAPS): These questions test your ability to follow physical/geographic directions using street maps or building maps. You will have to read and understand a set of directions and then use them on a simple map.

TEST TASK: You will be provided with street maps or building maps. You will then be asked questions which require you to refer to the given maps and related information.

SAMPLE QUESTION:

DIRECTIONS: Base your answer to the following question on the sample information and sample map below. The map below shows a section of a city. The circled numbers are starting points and stopping points. Buildings are shown with letters. A roadblock is shown as a dark circle. One-way blocks are shown with an arrow pointing in the direction that you may travel on that block. For example:

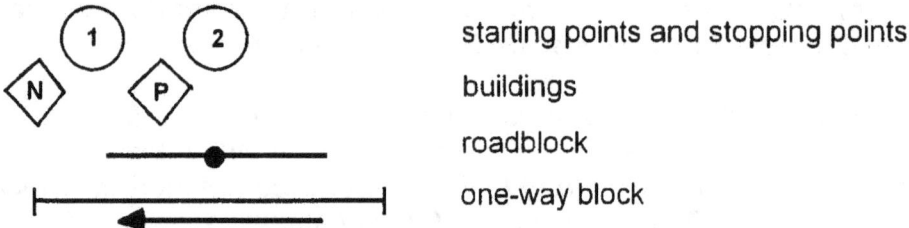

You may not go through a roadblock or travel in the wrong direction on a one-way block. You are to answer the question by finding and following the SHORTEST CORRECT route between the two locations given. All blocks are equal in length.

NOTE 1: Blocks may be traveled in either direction UNLESS only one direction is shown by an arrow for that block.

NOTE 2: You "pass" a building when you travel the block NEAREST the building.

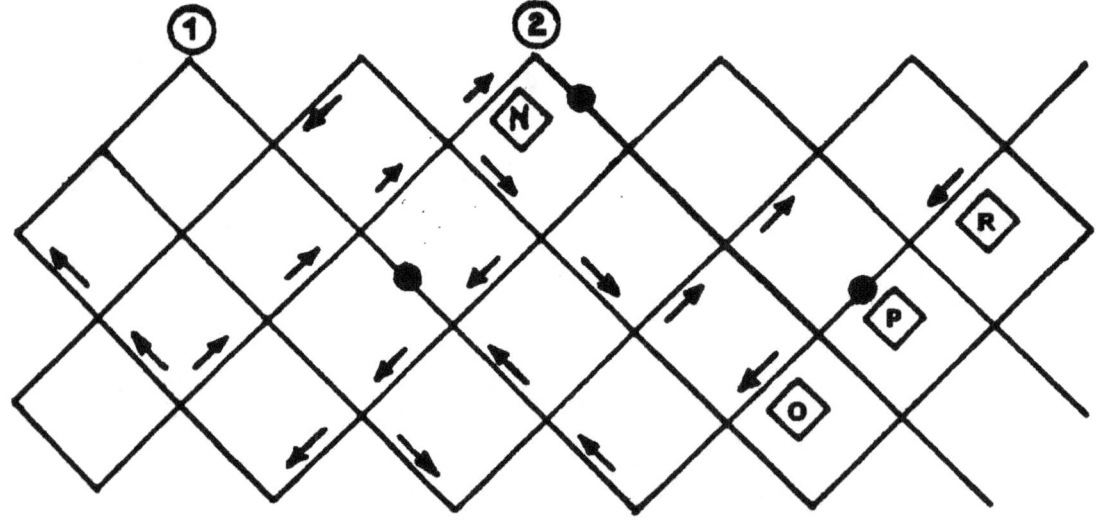

SUBJECT AREA 2 – CONTINUED

QUESTION: Which one of the following is a building you pass on the shortest correct route from point 1 to point 2?

A. N
B. O
C. P
D. R

The correct answer to this sample question is choice A.

SOLUTION:

Choice A *is the correct answer to this question. The shortest correct route from point 1 to point 2 is four blocks and passes only building N.*

Choice B *is not correct. You do not pass building O on the shortest correct route from point 1 to point 2.*

Choice C *is not correct. You do not pass building P on the shortest correct route from point 1 to point 2.*

Choice D *is not correct. You do not pass building R on the shortest correct route from point 1 to point 2.*

SUBJECT AREA 3

PREPARING WRITTEN MATERIAL: These questions test for the ability to present information clearly and accurately and for the ability to organize paragraphs logically and comprehensibly.

TEST TASK: There are two separate test tasks in this subject area.

- For the first, **Information Presentation**, you will be given information in two or three sentences, followed by four restatements of the information. You must then choose the best version.

- For the second, **Paragraph Organization**, you will be given paragraphs with their sentences out of order, and then be asked to choose, from among four choices, the best order for the sentences.

INFORMATION PRESENTATION SAMPLE QUESTION:

Martin Wilson failed to take proper precautions. His failure to take proper precautions caused a personal injury accident.

Which one of the following best presents the information above?

A. Martin Wilson failed to take proper precautions that caused a personal injury accident.
B. Proper precautions, which Martin Wilson failed to take, caused a personal injury accident.
C. Martin Wilson's failure to take proper precautions caused a personal injury accident.
D. Martin Wilson, who failed to take proper precautions, was in a personal injury accident.

The correct answer to this sample question is choice C.

SOLUTION:

Choice A *conveys the incorrect impression that proper precautions caused a personal injury accident.*

Choice B *conveys the incorrect impression that proper precautions caused a personal injury accident.*

Choice C *best presents the original information: Martin Wilson failed to take proper precautions and this failure caused a personal injury accident.*

Choice D *states that Martin Wilson was in a personal injury accident. The original information states that Martin Wilson caused a personal injury accident, but it does not state that Martin Wilson was in a personal injury accident.*

SUBJECT AREA 3 – CONTINUED

PARAGRAPH ORGANIZATION SAMPLE QUESTION:

The following question is based upon a group of sentences. The sentences are shown out of sequence, but when correctly arranged, they form a connected, well-organized paragraph. Read the sentences, and then answer the question about the best arrangement of these sentences.

1. Eventually, they piece all of this information together and make a choice.

2. Before actually deciding upon a human services job, people usually think about several possibilities.

3. They imagine themselves in different situations, and in so doing, they probably think about their interests, goals, and abilities.

4. Choosing among occupations in the field of human services is an important decision to make.

Which one of the following is the best arrangement of these sentences?

A. 2-4-1-3
B. 2-3-4-1
C. 4-2-1-3
D. 4-2-3-1

The correct answer to this sample question is choice D.

SOLUTION:

Choices A and C present the information in the paragraph out of logical sequence. In both A and C, sentence 1 comes before sentence 3. The key element in the organization of this paragraph is that sentence 3 contains the information to which sentence 1 refers; therefore, in logical sequence, sentence 3 should come before sentence 1.

Choice B also presents the information in the paragraph out of logical sequence. Choice B places the main idea of the paragraph (Sentence 4) in between two detail sentences (Sentences 1 and 3). The logical sequence of the information presented in the paragraph is therefore interrupted.

Choice D presents the information in the paragraph in the best logical sequence. Sentence 4 introduces the main idea of the paragraph: "choosing an occupation in the field of human services." Sentences 2-3-1 then follow up on this idea by describing, in order, the steps involved in making such a choice. Choice D is the best answer to this sample question.

SUBJECT AREA 4

PRINCIPLES AND PRACTICES OF SAFETY AND SECURITY: These questions test for a knowledge of the proper principles and practices in the field of safety and security. The questions will cover such areas as selecting the best course of action to take in a safety or security related situation.

TEST TASK: You will be presented with situations in which you must apply knowledge of the principles and practices of safety and security to answer the questions correctly.

SAMPLE QUESTION:

You are in charge of maintaining order in a room where a large number of people gather to transact business. A woman in the back of one of the lines starts to shout that she has been waiting for an hour and her line "has not moved at all." She continues to protest, and the rest of the crowd is getting restless.

Which one of the following actions would be best to take first in this situation?

A. Escort the woman to the head of the line and make sure her business is transacted promptly.
B. Tell the woman that unless she acts in a more orderly fashion, you will escort her out of the room.
C. Immediately remove the woman from the room.
D. Call the local police and detain the woman until the police arrive.

The correct answer to this sample question is choice B.

SOLUTION:

Choice A *is not correct because escorting the woman to the head of the line and making sure her business is transacted promptly is not the best action to take first in this situation. This action could increase the restlessness of the other people who have also been waiting in the same line and will only serve to reinforce the woman's disruptive behavior.*

Choice B *is the correct answer because telling the woman that unless she acts in a more orderly fashion, you will escort her out of the room is the best action to take first in this situation. This action provides the woman with a clear warning to stop her disruptive behavior and advises her of the consequence should she continue to loudly protest the long wait.*

Choice C *is not correct because immediately removing the woman from the room is not the best action to take first in this situation. This action is too harsh based on the situation and could escalate the woman's disruptive behavior.*

Choice D *is not correct because calling the local police and detaining the woman until they arrive is not the best action to take first in this situation. This action is too harsh based on the situation and could escalate the woman's disruptive behavior.*

SUBJECT AREA 5

SAFETY AND SECURITY METHODS AND PROCEDURES: These questions test for knowledge of the methods and procedures utilized in safety and security related positions. The questions cover such areas as principles and practices of safety and security precautions in a building or grounds setting, accident prevention, proper response to safety or security related incidents, the investigation of incidents, and the inspection of buildings or grounds for potential safety and/or security problems.

TEST TASK: You will be presented with questions in which you must apply knowledge of the methods and procedures utilized in safety and security related positions to answer the questions correctly.

SAMPLE QUESTION:

The most important purpose of patrolling the halls and grounds of a facility is to

A. discourage potential violations of rules or laws
B. give people on site the opportunity to obtain information or advice
C. maintain a routine observation of facility employees and their actions for your records
D. be able to provide assistance to local police authorities by accurately reporting whether unauthorized activity occurs in or near the facility

The correct answer to this sample question is choice A.

SOLUTION:

Choice A *is the correct answer because discouraging potential violations of rules or laws is the most important purpose of patrolling the halls and grounds of a facility. Your presence while patrolling the halls and grounds of a facility may be enough to deter potential rule or law violators.*

Choice B *is not correct because giving people on site the opportunity to obtain information or advice is not the most important purpose of patrolling the halls and grounds of a facility. Although giving people on site the opportunity to obtain information or advice may be an important purpose of patrolling the halls and grounds of a facility, it is not the most important purpose.*

Choice C *is not correct because maintaining a routine observation of facility employees and their actions for your records is not the most important purpose of patrolling the halls and grounds of a facility. Although maintaining a routine observation of facility employees and their actions for your records may be an important purpose of patrolling the halls and grounds of a facility, it is not the most important purpose.*

Choice D *is not correct because being able to provide assistance to local police authorities by accurately reporting whether unauthorized activity occurs in or near the facility is not the most important purpose of patrolling the halls and grounds of a facility. Although being able to provide assistance to local police authorities by accurately reporting whether unauthorized activity occurs in or near the facility may be an important purpose of patrolling the halls and grounds of a facility, it is not the most important purpose.*

SUBJECT AREA 6

UNDERSTANDING AND INTERPRETING WRITTEN MATERIAL: These questions test how well you comprehend written material. You will be provided with brief reading selections and will be asked questions about the selections. All the information required to answer the questions will be presented in the selections; you will not be required to have any special knowledge relating to the subject areas of the selections.

TEST TASK: You will be provided with brief reading passages and then will be asked questions relating to the passages. All the information required to answer the questions will be provided in the passages.

SAMPLE QUESTION: "Increasingly, behavior termed 'road rage' is being viewed as a public health issue, because of the number of deaths and injuries related to it. Such behavior is often a reaction to the feeling that one has been treated unfairly by another driver, and it is much less likely to occur if a driver is treated fairly. 'Fair play' on the road includes the observance not only of traffic regulations but also of the rules of courtesy. Courteous driving is based on common sense consideration for other drivers and a strong desire to make the roads safe for everyone. Good highway manners should become just as much a matter of habit as other kinds of manners."

Which one of the following statements is best supported by the above selection?

A. Courteous driving contributes to road safety.
B. Those who are generally polite are also courteous drivers.
C. Unlike driving courtesy, the observance of traffic regulations is a matter of habit.
D. Being courteous when driving is more important than observing traffic regulations.

The correct answer to this sample question is choice A.

SOLUTION: To answer this question correctly, you must evaluate each choice against the written selection and determine the one that is best supported by the written selection.

Choice A states, *"Courteous driving contributes to road safety."* Choice A is supported by the statement in the written selection that, "Courteous driving is based on...a strong desire to make the roads safe for everyone." This is the correct answer.

Choice B states, *"Those who are generally polite are also courteous drivers."* Choice B is not supported by the written selection. The written selection does not mention "those who are generally polite" at all. Choice B is not the correct answer to this question.

Choice C states, *"Unlike driving courtesy, the observance of traffic regulations is a matter of habit."* Choice C is not supported by the written selection. The written selection makes no such bold statement. Instead, the written material mildly suggests that "Good highway manners should become just as much a matter of habit as other kinds of manners." Choice C is not the correct answer to this question.

Choice D states, *"Being courteous when driving is more important than observing traffic regulations."* Choice D is not supported by the written selection. The written selection states, "'Fair play' on the road includes the observance not only of traffic regulations but also of the rules of courtesy." The written selection does not state that being courteous is more important than observing traffic regulations. Choice D is not the correct answer to this question.

SUBJECT AREA 7

SUPERVISION: These questions test for knowledge of the principles and practices employed in planning, organizing, and controlling the activities of a work unit toward predetermined objectives. The concepts covered, usually in a situational question format, include such topics as assigning and reviewing work; evaluating performance; maintaining work standards; motivating and developing subordinates; implementing procedural change; increasing efficiency; and dealing with problems of absenteeism, morale, and discipline.

TEST TASK: You will be presented with situations in which you must apply knowledge of the principles and practices of supervision in order to answer the questions correctly.

SAMPLE QUESTION:
Assume that the unit you supervise is given a new work assignment and that you are unsure about the proper procedure to use in performing this assignment. Which one of the following actions should you take FIRST in this situation?

A. Obtain input from your staff.
B. Consult other unit supervisors who have had similar assignments.
C. Use an appropriate procedure from a similar assignment that you are familiar with.
D. Discuss the matter with your supervisor.

The correct answer to this sample question is choice D.

SOLUTION:

Choice A is not correct. Since this assignment is new for your unit, your staff would not be expected to be more knowledgeable than you about the proper procedure.

Choice B is not correct. Although discussing this matter with other supervisors may increase your knowledge of the new assignment, similar assignments performed in other units may differ in some important way from your new assignment. Other units may also function differently from your unit, so the procedures used to perform similar assignments may differ accordingly.

Choice C is not correct. Since this assignment is new for your unit, you would have no way of knowing whether the procedure from a similar assignment is appropriate to use. You would need someone with the appropriate knowledge, usually your supervisor, to determine if the procedure from a similar assignment could be used before you actually employed this procedure in the performance of your new assignment.

Choice D is the correct answer to this question. Your supervisor is more likely to be informed about what procedure may be appropriate for work that he or she assigns to you than would other unit supervisors or your staff. Even if your supervisor does not know what procedure is appropriate, a decision regarding which procedure to use should be made with his or her participation, since he or she has the ultimate responsibility for your unit's work.

SUBJECT AREA 8

ADMINISTRATIVE SUPERVISION: These questions test for knowledge of the principles and practices involved in directing the activities of a large subordinate staff, including subordinate supervisors. Questions relate to the personal interactions between an upper level supervisor and his/her subordinate supervisors in the accomplishment of objectives. These questions cover such areas as assigning work to and coordinating the activities of several units, establishing and guiding staff development programs, evaluating the performance of subordinate supervisors, and maintaining relationships with other organizational sections.

TEST TASK: You will be presented with situations in which you must apply knowledge of the principles and practices of administrative supervision to answer the questions correctly. You will be placed in the role of a supervisor of a section, which is made up of several units. Each unit has a supervisor and several employees. All unit supervisors report directly to you.

SAMPLE QUESTION:

You have delegated a work project to two unit supervisors and have asked them to collaborate on it. Later, you observe two employees strongly arguing about which one of them is responsible for a certain activity within the work project. The arguing employees work for different units. Which one of the following actions is most appropriate for you to take in this situation?

A. Intercede in the employees' argument and settle it.
B. Meet with the unit supervisors of the two employees and inform them of the situation you observed.
C. Inform one unit supervisor of the situation and ask this supervisor to take care of it.
D. Set up a meeting that includes both unit supervisors and both employees to resolve the situation.

The correct answer to this sample question is choice B.

SOLUTION:

Choice A is not correct. In your position, you supervise properly by giving direction through your unit supervisors. By taking this choice, you are not allowing your unit supervisors to handle a problem involving their staff members. Also, it is not reasonable that you would be able to settle the employees' dispute. Earlier, you delegated the work project to the two unit supervisors, who would be responsible for assigning activities related to the project. The two unit supervisors must deal with the problem.

Choice B is the correct answer to this question. The two unit supervisors are collaborating on the work project and therefore giving the assignments. You should meet with them and tell them about the employees' argument. The unit supervisors should be informed about the point of contention and the fact that the two employees had a heated argument. The unit supervisors must then work out a way to handle the situation.

Choice C is not correct. Speaking to only one supervisor about the situation means that the second supervisor may be uninformed, or only partly informed, about the situation. You cannot be assured that the first supervisor will include the second supervisor in finding a way to settle the issue. If the first unit supervisor chooses to handle the situation on his own and speak to both employees, this supervisor would be giving direction to one employee from another unit. This is not good supervisory practice. Also, in taking Choice C, you are favoring one supervisor and slighting the other.

Choice D is not correct. The unit supervisors need to come up with a way of handling the situation that you observed. To do this, they must be informed without the employees present. Also, by including the employees in the meeting, you may get a replay of their earlier argument, which is not helpful.

PRACTICE TEST

Below and on the following pages are additional examples of the types of questions that will be on the written test for the Safety and Security Series. The answers are given on page 25. Good luck!

APPLYING WRITTEN INFORMATION IN A SAFETY AND SECURITY SETTING

DIRECTIONS: The following two questions evaluate your ability to read and interpret a specific rule and apply it to a given situation or situations. Each question or set of questions is given with a **RULE** along with a **SITUATION** or situations. You should base your answers to these questions upon the information provided and **NOT** upon any other information you may have on the subject.

1. **RULE:** A security officer is to obey all lawful regulations of the employer and all orders of a police officer in police matters. The security officer is to assist and cooperate with police officers in preserving the peace. Where police are on the scene, on duty and off duty security personnel should identify themselves as security officers and offer assistance. The police officer's directives and judgment shall prevail.

SITUATION: When leaving work for the day, you see that a motor vehicle accident has taken place on the highway near your workplace. You approach the accident in your car and see that a police officer is on the scene. You inform the police officer that you are a security officer. Traffic is stopped.

According to the above Rule, under which one of the following conditions, if any, should you take control of directing traffic in this Situation?

A. The police officer instructs you to direct traffic.
B. You regularly direct traffic as part of your job.
C. You should not direct traffic because you are off duty.
D. You should not direct traffic because the highway is not on facility property.

2. **RULE:** If a law enforcement officer is required to be at a mental health facility, the officer will be required to lock his weapon in a designated gun cabinet and retain the only key. In areas where gun cabinets are not available, the law enforcement officer shall be asked to remove the bullets from his weapon and retain the weapon. The only other allowable option is for the officer to lock the weapon in his patrol car.

SITUATION: During rounds as a security officer in a mental health facility with no gun control cabinets available, you come upon a law enforcement officer whom you know to be a firearms instructor. You allow the officer to enter the building with his weapon.

Based solely on the above Rule and Situation, in which one of the following cases is your action correct?

A. The officer has stated that his police agency prohibits an officer from locking a weapon in his patrol car.
B. The officer has stated that he would be willing to put his weapon in a gun cabinet.
C. The officer has shown you a letter stating he must attend a meeting at the facility today on the topic of firearm instruction.
D. The officer has removed the bullets from his weapon.

FOLLOWING DIRECTIONS (MAPS)

DIRECTIONS: The following map presents a diagram of a floor of an office building. You should become familiar with the map and interpret it with the legend provided. Use the map to answer the questions on the next page.

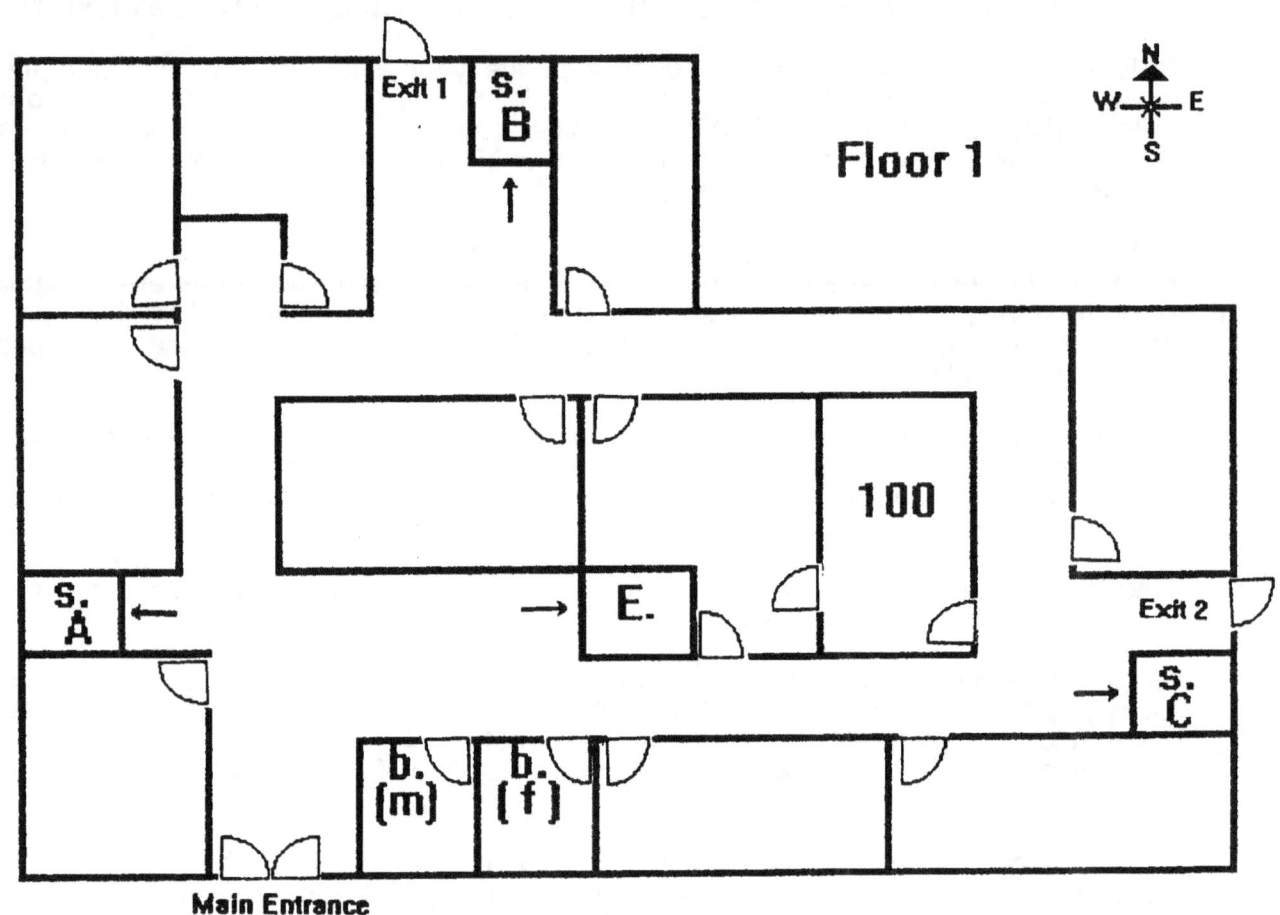

Legend:

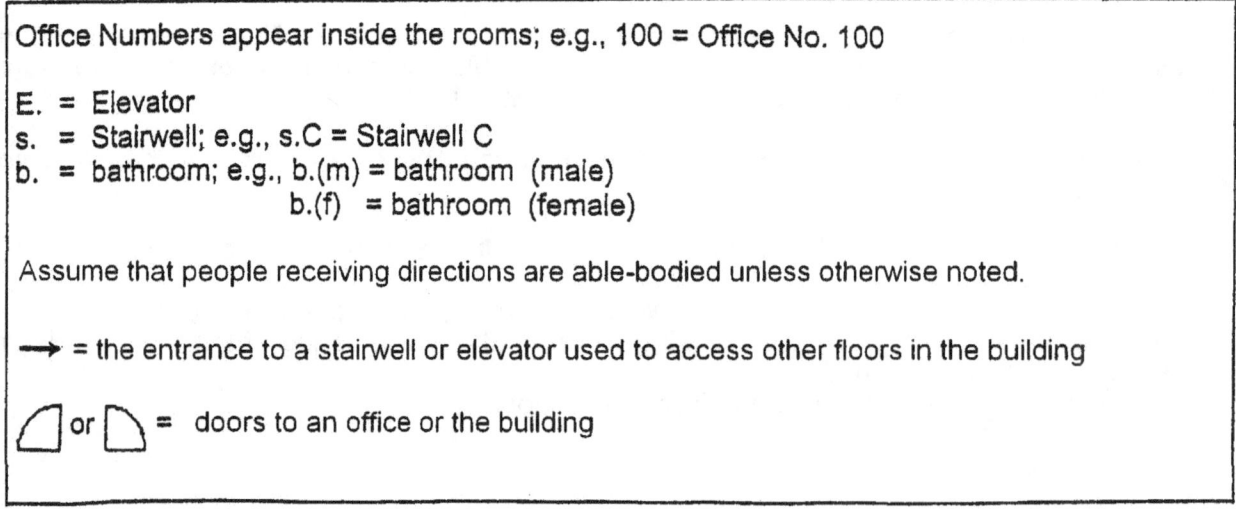

FOLLOWING DIRECTIONS (MAPS) (Continued)

3. For a person in Office No. 100, which one of the following is the most direct route to leave the building in an emergency?

A. through exit 1
B. through exit 2
C. through stairwell C
D. through the Main Entrance

4. Which one of the following routes is the best to take if the elevator is out of service and a person standing directly inside the main entrance wants to get from Floor 1 to Floor 2 in the most efficient way?

A. Walk straight, take the second right, take the first left and take stairwell B to the second floor.
B. Walk straight, take the second right, walk straight, take the next right, take the first left and take stairwell C to the second floor.
C. Walk straight, take the first right, walk straight and take stairwell C to the second floor.
D. Walk straight, take the first left and take stairwell A to the second floor.

PREPARING WRITTEN MATERIAL

DIRECTIONS: Read the information given in the following two questions carefully. Then select the choice which presents the information most clearly, accurately, and completely.

5. Senator Martinez met with the county legislature. Then Senator Martinez announced that the meal subsidy program would start in June.

Which one of the following best presents the information given above?

A. After meeting with the county legislature, Senator Martinez announced that the meal subsidy program would start in June.
B. Senator Martinez met with the county legislature and announced that the meal subsidy program would start in June.
C. Senator Martinez announced that the meal subsidy program would start in June after a meeting with the county legislature.
D. Senator Martinez, who met with the county legislature, announced that the meal subsidy program would start in June.

6. Frank Colombe wrote the press release. He sent three copies to the Director. The Director then gave one of the copies to the Commissioner.

Which one of the following best presents the information given above?

A. Frank Colombe sent to the Director three copies of the press release he had written, who then gave a copy to the Commissioner.
B. Frank Colombe sent three copies of the press release he had written to the Director, who then gave one of the copies to the Commissioner.
C. The Director gave the Commissioner one of the three copies of the press release Frank Colombe had written and had been sent to him.
D. Of the three copies of the press release Frank Colombe had written and sent to the Director, one was then given to the Commissioner by him.

PREPARING WRITTEN MATERIAL (Continued)

DIRECTIONS: The following two (2) questions are based upon a group of sentences. The sentences are shown out of sequence, but when they are correctly arranged they form a connected, well-organized paragraph. Read the sentences and then answer the question about what order to arrange them in.

7.
1. The phosphates in detergents are carried into sewage systems, and from there into local rivers and streams, and eventually into large bodies of water.

2. The algae absorb much of the available oxygen that is necessary to sustain marine life.

3. There is no doubt that phosphates damage the environment through a complex chain of events.

4. Phosphates are nutrients, and, as such, they aid the growth of the algae living in the water.

5. This results not only in the death of fish and other aquatic life, but also in the too-thick growth of vegetation in the water.

Which one of the following is the best arrangement of these sentences?

A. 1-3-4-2-5
B. 1-4-2-5-3
C. 3-1-4-2-5
D. 3-4-2-1-5

8.
1. Never before has time been measured at a speed beyond the realm of experience.

2. Just how profound an effect it is having on society is as yet to be determined.

3. The computer has accelerated our sense of time beyond anything we have experienced before.

4. Though it is possible to conceive of an interval that brief and even to manipulate time at that speed, it is not possible to experience it.

5. It works in a time frame in which the nanosecond—a billionth of a second—is the primary measurement.

Which one of the following is the best arrangement of these sentences?

A. 1-2-3-5-4
B. 1-4-3-5-2
C. 3-2-5-4-1
D. 3-5-4-1-2

PRINCIPLES AND PRACTICES OF SAFETY AND SECURITY

9. You are on patrol in a radio-equipped car at night. You discover that a large drum of gasoline near a garage on the property is punctured and is rapidly spilling gasoline on the ground around the building.

Which one of the following actions should you take first in this situation?

A. Submit a written report of the incident to your supervisor.
B. Report the matter to headquarters.
C. Examine the puncture to see if it was accidental or deliberate.
D. Check other drums or containers around the building for punctures.

10. You hear shouting on the second floor of a building where you are on duty. Upon arriving at the scene, you see two building employees engaged in a fist fight in the hall.

Which one of the following actions should you take first in this situation?

A. Report the matter to the supervisors of the two employees.
B. Ask observers how the fight started.
C. Call for assistance.
D. Break up the fight.

SAFETY AND SECURITY METHODS AND PROCEDURES

11. Complaints relating to suspicious activity, especially at night, are often groundless. Which one of the following is the best way of handling such a complaint?

A. Analyze the nature of the complaint to make sure that it is justifiable before dispatching anyone to the scene.
B. Consider the complaint justified only if it corresponds to similar complaints in the same area.
C. Take no action on the complaint, but make a record of it.
D. Attend to the complaint immediately on the assumption that it is justified.

12. In the course of an investigation, you are interviewing a person who is over-talkative. Which one of the following is the best method for you to use in order to obtain the facts which you seek?

A. Tell the witness to talk only about the facts you are interested in.
B. Place a time limit on the witness's answers to your questions.
C. Make it clear that you want only "yes" or "no" answers to your questions.
D. Guide the conversation toward the subject of interest when the witness talks about subjects clearly not relevant to the interview.

UNDERSTANDING AND INTERPRETING WRITTEN MATERIAL

DIRECTIONS: The following two questions are related to the reading selection preceding each question. Base your answer to the question SOLELY on what is said in the selection – NOT on what you may happen to know about the subject discussed.

13. "The increasing demands upon our highways from a growing population and the development of forms of transportation not anticipated when the highways were first built have brought about congestion, confusion, and conflict, until the yearly toll of traffic accidents is now at an appalling level. If the death and disaster that traffic accidents bring throughout the year were concentrated into one calamity, we would shudder at the tremendous catastrophe. The loss is no less catastrophic because it is spread out over time and space."

Which one of the following statements concerning the yearly toll of traffic accidents is best supported by the passage above?

A. It is increasing the demands for safer means of transportation.
B. It has resulted in increased congestion, confusion, and conflict on our highways.
C. It has resulted mainly from the new forms of transportation.
D. It does not shock us as much as it should because the accidents do not all occur at the same time.

14. "Depression is one of the top public health problems in the United States, and its occurrence is on the rise. One in 20 Americans develops a case of depression serious enough to require professional treatment. The incidence of depression has been escalating among Baby Boomers (Americans born in the years 1946 through 1964). The reason for this increase is that the lifestyles of this generation have become increasingly demanding while offering little support. Also, stress and poor eating habits are now more the rule than the exception, and both can disrupt brain chemistry enough to bring on depression."

Which one of the following statements is best supported by the above selection?

A. We can expect a small proportion of the population to require treatment for depression at some time in their lives.
B. Baby Boomers have the highest rate of depression in the United States.
C. Lifestyle demands are the major cause of depression in the current generation.
D. Depression can cause a disruption in the chemistry of the brain.

SUPERVISION

DIRECTIONS: For the following two questions, assume that you are the newly appointed supervisor of a unit consisting of several employees. You report to a section head.

15. You have a suspicion that some of your employees are not working to the best of their abilities. Which one of the following actions should you take first in this situation?

A. Arrange for these employees to take a course in organizing priorities.
B. Determine which employee is the worst offender.
C. Assess the assignments and work methods of these employees.
D. Set up a meeting with these employees to learn about any work problems they are having.

16. As you are giving an employee a certain assignment, she expresses concern that it is too difficult. The employee is reluctant to accept the assignment. Which one of the following actions should you take first in this situation?

A. Insist that the employee take on the assignment.
B. Tell the employee that it is likely she has completed assignments of similar difficulty before.
C. Offer to share the tasks of the assignment with the employee.
D. Ask the employee why she sees the assignment as difficult.

ADMINISTRATIVE SUPERVISION

DIRECTIONS: For the following two questions, assume that you supervise a section composed of several units. Each unit has a supervisor and several employees. All unit supervisors report directly to you.

17. Assume that you are the head of a section made up of four units, each of which is responsible for similar work. The work volume of one of the units of the section has permanently decreased to the point that the supervisor of that unit now is responsible for much less work than any of the other three unit supervisors. Of the following, which determination should you as the section head make first in this situation?

A. Can other or additional tasks be assigned to this unit?
B. Can the unit supervisor function as assistant section head?
C. Can the unit supervisor's position be reclassified or reallocated?
D. Can the section be reorganized into three units?

18. In which one of the following circumstances should you try to reduce turnover in the section you supervise?

A. The turnover is higher than that of other sections.
B. The turnover reduces the number of highly experienced employees.
C. The turnover lowers the efficiency of the section.
D. The turnover requires unit supervisors to spend a moderate amount of time in training new employees.

PRACTICE TEST KEY

(1) A
(2) D
(3) B
(4) D
(5) A
(6) B
(7) C
(8) D
(9) B
(10) C
(11) D
(12) D
(13) D
(14) A
(15) C
(16) D
(17) A
(18) C

HOW TO TAKE A TEST

I. YOU MUST PASS AN EXAMINATION

A. *WHAT EVERY CANDIDATE SHOULD KNOW*

    Examination applicants often ask us for help in preparing for the written test. What can I study in advance? What kinds of questions will be asked? How will the test be given? How will the papers be graded?

    As an applicant for a civil service examination, you may be wondering about some of these things. Our purpose here is to suggest effective methods of advance study and to describe civil service examinations.

    Your chances for success on this examination can be increased if you know how to prepare. Those "pre-examination jitters" can be reduced if you know what to expect. You can even experience an adventure in good citizenship if you know why civil service exams are given.

B. *WHY ARE CIVIL SERVICE EXAMINATIONS GIVEN?*

    Civil service examinations are important to you in two ways. As a citizen, you want public jobs filled by employees who know how to do their work. As a job seeker, you want a fair chance to compete for that job on an equal footing with other candidates. The best-known means of accomplishing this two-fold goal is the competitive examination.

    Exams are widely publicized throughout the nation. They may be administered for jobs in federal, state, city, municipal, town or village governments or agencies.

    Any citizen may apply, with some limitations, such as the age or residence of applicants. Your experience and education may be reviewed to see whether you meet the requirements for the particular examination. When these requirements exist, they are reasonable and applied consistently to all applicants. Thus, a competitive examination may cause you some uneasiness now, but it is your privilege and safeguard.

C. *HOW ARE CIVIL SERVICE EXAMS DEVELOPED?*

    Examinations are carefully written by trained technicians who are specialists in the field known as "psychological measurement," in consultation with recognized authorities in the field of work that the test will cover. These experts recommend the subject matter areas or skills to be tested; only those knowledges or skills important to your success on the job are included. The most reliable books and source materials available are used as references. Together, the experts and technicians judge the difficulty level of the questions.

    Test technicians know how to phrase questions so that the problem is clearly stated. Their ethics do not permit "trick" or "catch" questions. Questions may have been tried out on sample groups, or subjected to statistical analysis, to determine their usefulness.

    Written tests are often used in combination with performance tests, ratings of training and experience, and oral interviews. All of these measures combine to form the best-known means of finding the right person for the right job.

II. HOW TO PASS THE WRITTEN TEST

A. NATURE OF THE EXAMINATION

To prepare intelligently for civil service examinations, you should know how they differ from school examinations you have taken. In school you were assigned certain definite pages to read or subjects to cover. The examination questions were quite detailed and usually emphasized memory. Civil service exams, on the other hand, try to discover your present ability to perform the duties of a position, plus your potentiality to learn these duties. In other words, a civil service exam attempts to predict how successful you will be. Questions cover such a broad area that they cannot be as minute and detailed as school exam questions.

In the public service similar kinds of work, or positions, are grouped together in one "class." This process is known as *position-classification*. All the positions in a class are paid according to the salary range for that class. One class title covers all of these positions, and they are all tested by the same examination.

B. FOUR BASIC STEPS

1) Study the announcement

How, then, can you know what subjects to study? Our best answer is: "Learn as much as possible about the class of positions for which you've applied." The exam will test the knowledge, skills and abilities needed to do the work.

Your most valuable source of information about the position you want is the official exam announcement. This announcement lists the training and experience qualifications. Check these standards and apply only if you come reasonably close to meeting them.

The brief description of the position in the examination announcement offers some clues to the subjects which will be tested. Think about the job itself. Review the duties in your mind. Can you perform them, or are there some in which you are rusty? Fill in the blank spots in your preparation.

Many jurisdictions preview the written test in the exam announcement by including a section called "Knowledge and Abilities Required," "Scope of the Examination," or some similar heading. Here you will find out specifically what fields will be tested.

2) Review your own background

Once you learn in general what the position is all about, and what you need to know to do the work, ask yourself which subjects you already know fairly well and which need improvement. You may wonder whether to concentrate on improving your strong areas or on building some background in your fields of weakness. When the announcement has specified "some knowledge" or "considerable knowledge," or has used adjectives like "beginning principles of..." or "advanced ... methods," you can get a clue as to the number and difficulty of questions to be asked in any given field. More questions, and hence broader coverage, would be included for those subjects which are more important in the work. Now weigh your strengths and weaknesses against the job requirements and prepare accordingly.

3) Determine the level of the position

Another way to tell how intensively you should prepare is to understand the level of the job for which you are applying. Is it the entering level? In other words, is this the position in which beginners in a field of work are hired? Or is it an intermediate or advanced level? Sometimes this is indicated by such words as "Junior" or "Senior" in the class title. Other jurisdictions use Roman numerals to designate the level – Clerk I, Clerk II, for example. The word "Supervisor" sometimes appears in the title. If the level is not indicated by the title, check the description of duties. Will you be working under very close supervision, or will you have responsibility for independent decisions in this work?

4) Choose appropriate study materials

Now that you know the subjects to be examined and the relative amount of each subject to be covered, you can choose suitable study materials. For beginning level jobs, or even advanced ones, if you have a pronounced weakness in some aspect of your training, read a modern, standard textbook in that field. Be sure it is up to date and has general coverage. Such books are normally available at your library, and the librarian will be glad to help you locate one. For entry-level positions, questions of appropriate difficulty are chosen -- neither highly advanced questions, nor those too simple. Such questions require careful thought but not advanced training.

If the position for which you are applying is technical or advanced, you will read more advanced, specialized material. If you are already familiar with the basic principles of your field, elementary textbooks would waste your time. Concentrate on advanced textbooks and technical periodicals. Think through the concepts and review difficult problems in your field.

These are all general sources. You can get more ideas on your own initiative, following these leads. For example, training manuals and publications of the government agency which employs workers in your field can be useful, particularly for technical and professional positions. A letter or visit to the government department involved may result in more specific study suggestions, and certainly will provide you with a more definite idea of the exact nature of the position you are seeking.

III. KINDS OF TESTS

Tests are used for purposes other than measuring knowledge and ability to perform specified duties. For some positions, it is equally important to test ability to make adjustments to new situations or to profit from training. In others, basic mental abilities not dependent on information are essential. Questions which test these things may not appear as pertinent to the duties of the position as those which test for knowledge and information. Yet they are often highly important parts of a fair examination. For very general questions, it is almost impossible to help you direct your study efforts. What we can do is to point out some of the more common of these general abilities needed in public service positions and describe some typical questions.

1) General information

Broad, general information has been found useful for predicting job success in some kinds of work. This is tested in a variety of ways, from vocabulary lists to questions about current events. Basic background in some field of work, such as sociology or economics, may be sampled in a group of questions. Often these are principles which have become familiar to most persons through exposure rather than through formal training. It is difficult to advise you how to study for these questions; being alert to the world around you is our best suggestion.

2) Verbal ability

An example of an ability needed in many positions is verbal or language ability. Verbal ability is, in brief, the ability to use and understand words. Vocabulary and grammar tests are typical measures of this ability. Reading comprehension or paragraph interpretation questions are common in many kinds of civil service tests. You are given a paragraph of written material and asked to find its central meaning.

3) Numerical ability

Number skills can be tested by the familiar arithmetic problem, by checking paired lists of numbers to see which are alike and which are different, or by interpreting charts and graphs. In the latter test, a graph may be printed in the test booklet which you are asked to use as the basis for answering questions.

4) Observation

A popular test for law-enforcement positions is the observation test. A picture is shown to you for several minutes, then taken away. Questions about the picture test your ability to observe both details and larger elements.

5) Following directions

In many positions in the public service, the employee must be able to carry out written instructions dependably and accurately. You may be given a chart with several columns, each column listing a variety of information. The questions require you to carry out directions involving the information given in the chart.

6) Skills and aptitudes

Performance tests effectively measure some manual skills and aptitudes. When the skill is one in which you are trained, such as typing or shorthand, you can practice. These tests are often very much like those given in business school or high school courses. For many of the other skills and aptitudes, however, no short-time preparation can be made. Skills and abilities natural to you or that you have developed throughout your lifetime are being tested.

Many of the general questions just described provide all the data needed to answer the questions and ask you to use your reasoning ability to find the answers. Your best preparation for these tests, as well as for tests of facts and ideas, is to be at your physical and mental best. You, no doubt, have your own methods of getting into an exam-taking mood and keeping "in shape." The next section lists some ideas on this subject.

IV. KINDS OF QUESTIONS

Only rarely is the "essay" question, which you answer in narrative form, used in civil service tests. Civil service tests are usually of the short-answer type. Full instructions for answering these questions will be given to you at the examination. But in case this is your first experience with short-answer questions and separate answer sheets, here is what you need to know:

1) Multiple-choice Questions

Most popular of the short-answer questions is the "multiple choice" or "best answer" question. It can be used, for example, to test for factual knowledge, ability to solve problems or judgment in meeting situations found at work.

A multiple-choice question is normally one of three types—

- It can begin with an incomplete statement followed by several possible endings. You are to find the one ending which *best* completes the statement, although some of the others may not be entirely wrong.
- It can also be a complete statement in the form of a question which is answered by choosing one of the statements listed.

- It can be in the form of a problem – again you select the best answer.

Here is an example of a multiple-choice question with a discussion which should give you some clues as to the method for choosing the right answer:

When an employee has a complaint about his assignment, the action which will *best* help him overcome his difficulty is to
    A. discuss his difficulty with his coworkers
    B. take the problem to the head of the organization
    C. take the problem to the person who gave him the assignment
    D. say nothing to anyone about his complaint

In answering this question, you should study each of the choices to find which is best. Consider choice "A" – Certainly an employee may discuss his complaint with fellow employees, but no change or improvement can result, and the complaint remains unresolved. Choice "B" is a poor choice since the head of the organization probably does not know what assignment you have been given, and taking your problem to him is known as "going over the head" of the supervisor. The supervisor, or person who made the assignment, is the person who can clarify it or correct any injustice. Choice "C" is, therefore, correct. To say nothing, as in choice "D," is unwise. Supervisors have and interest in knowing the problems employees are facing, and the employee is seeking a solution to his problem.

2) True/False Questions

The "true/false" or "right/wrong" form of question is sometimes used. Here a complete statement is given. Your job is to decide whether the statement is right or wrong.

SAMPLE: A roaming cell-phone call to a nearby city costs less than a non-roaming call to a distant city.

This statement is wrong, or false, since roaming calls are more expensive.

This is not a complete list of all possible question forms, although most of the others are variations of these common types. You will always get complete directions for answering questions. Be sure you understand *how* to mark your answers – ask questions until you do.

V. RECORDING YOUR ANSWERS

Computer terminals are used more and more today for many different kinds of exams.
For an examination with very few applicants, you may be told to record your answers in the test booklet itself. Separate answer sheets are much more common. If this separate answer sheet is to be scored by machine – and this is often the case – it is highly important that you mark your answers correctly in order to get credit.

An electronic scoring machine is often used in civil service offices because of the speed with which papers can be scored. Machine-scored answer sheets must be marked with a pencil, which will be given to you. This pencil has a high graphite content which responds to the electronic scoring machine. As a matter of fact, stray dots may register as answers, so do not let your pencil rest on the answer sheet while you are pondering the correct answer. Also, if your pencil lead breaks or is otherwise defective, ask for another.

Since the answer sheet will be dropped in a slot in the scoring machine, be careful not to bend the corners or get the paper crumpled.

The answer sheet normally has five vertical columns of numbers, with 30 numbers to a column. These numbers correspond to the question numbers in your test booklet. After each number, going across the page are four or five pairs of dotted lines. These short dotted lines have small letters or numbers above them. The first two pairs may also have a "T" or "F" above the letters. This indicates that the first two pairs only are to be used if the questions are of the true-false type. If the questions are multiple choice, disregard the "T" and "F" and pay attention only to the small letters or numbers.

Answer your questions in the manner of the sample that follows:

32. The largest city in the United States is
    A. Washington, D.C.
    B. New York City
    C. Chicago
    D. Detroit
    E. San Francisco

1) Choose the answer you think is best. (New York City is the largest, so "B" is correct.)
2) Find the row of dotted lines numbered the same as the question you are answering. (Find row number 32)
3) Find the pair of dotted lines corresponding to the answer. (Find the pair of lines under the mark "B.")
4) Make a solid black mark between the dotted lines.

VI. BEFORE THE TEST

Common sense will help you find procedures to follow to get ready for an examination. Too many of us, however, overlook these sensible measures. Indeed, nervousness and fatigue have been found to be the most serious reasons why applicants fail to do their best on civil service tests. Here is a list of reminders:

- Begin your preparation early – Don't wait until the last minute to go scurrying around for books and materials or to find out what the position is all about.
- Prepare continuously – An hour a night for a week is better than an all-night cram session. This has been definitely established. What is more, a night a week for a month will return better dividends than crowding your study into a shorter period of time.
- Locate the place of the exam – You have been sent a notice telling you when and where to report for the examination. If the location is in a different town or otherwise unfamiliar to you, it would be well to inquire the best route and learn something about the building.
- Relax the night before the test – Allow your mind to rest. Do not study at all that night. Plan some mild recreation or diversion; then go to bed early and get a good night's sleep.
- Get up early enough to make a leisurely trip to the place for the test – This way unforeseen events, traffic snarls, unfamiliar buildings, etc. will not upset you.
- Dress comfortably – A written test is not a fashion show. You will be known by number and not by name, so wear something comfortable.

- Leave excess paraphernalia at home – Shopping bags and odd bundles will get in your way. You need bring only the items mentioned in the official notice you received; usually everything you need is provided. Do not bring reference books to the exam. They will only confuse those last minutes and be taken away from you when in the test room.
- Arrive somewhat ahead of time – If because of transportation schedules you must get there very early, bring a newspaper or magazine to take your mind off yourself while waiting.
- Locate the examination room – When you have found the proper room, you will be directed to the seat or part of the room where you will sit. Sometimes you are given a sheet of instructions to read while you are waiting. Do not fill out any forms until you are told to do so; just read them and be prepared.
- Relax and prepare to listen to the instructions
- If you have any physical problem that may keep you from doing your best, be sure to tell the test administrator. If you are sick or in poor health, you really cannot do your best on the exam. You can come back and take the test some other time.

VII. AT THE TEST

The day of the test is here and you have the test booklet in your hand. The temptation to get going is very strong. Caution! There is more to success than knowing the right answers. You must know how to identify your papers and understand variations in the type of short-answer question used in this particular examination. Follow these suggestions for maximum results from your efforts:

1) Cooperate with the monitor

The test administrator has a duty to create a situation in which you can be as much at ease as possible. He will give instructions, tell you when to begin, check to see that you are marking your answer sheet correctly, and so on. He is not there to guard you, although he will see that your competitors do not take unfair advantage. He wants to help you do your best.

2) Listen to all instructions

Don't jump the gun! Wait until you understand all directions. In most civil service tests you get more time than you need to answer the questions. So don't be in a hurry. Read each word of instructions until you clearly understand the meaning. Study the examples, listen to all announcements and follow directions. Ask questions if you do not understand what to do.

3) Identify your papers

Civil service exams are usually identified by number only. You will be assigned a number; you must not put your name on your test papers. Be sure to copy your number correctly. Since more than one exam may be given, copy your exact examination title.

4) Plan your time

Unless you are told that a test is a "speed" or "rate of work" test, speed itself is usually not important. Time enough to answer all the questions will be provided, but this does not mean that you have all day. An overall time limit has been set. Divide the total time (in minutes) by the number of questions to determine the approximate time you have for each question.

5) Do not linger over difficult questions

If you come across a difficult question, mark it with a paper clip (useful to have along) and come back to it when you have been through the booklet. One caution if you do this – be sure to skip a number on your answer sheet as well. Check often to be sure that you have not lost your place and that you are marking in the row numbered the same as the question you are answering.

6) Read the questions

Be sure you know what the question asks! Many capable people are unsuccessful because they failed to *read* the questions correctly.

7) Answer all questions

Unless you have been instructed that a penalty will be deducted for incorrect answers, it is better to guess than to omit a question.

8) Speed tests

It is often better NOT to guess on speed tests. It has been found that on timed tests people are tempted to spend the last few seconds before time is called in marking answers at random – without even reading them – in the hope of picking up a few extra points. To discourage this practice, the instructions may warn you that your score will be "corrected" for guessing. That is, a penalty will be applied. The incorrect answers will be deducted from the correct ones, or some other penalty formula will be used.

9) Review your answers

If you finish before time is called, go back to the questions you guessed or omitted to give them further thought. Review other answers if you have time.

10) Return your test materials

If you are ready to leave before others have finished or time is called, take ALL your materials to the monitor and leave quietly. Never take any test material with you. The monitor can discover whose papers are not complete, and taking a test booklet may be grounds for disqualification.

VIII. EXAMINATION TECHNIQUES

1) Read the general instructions carefully. These are usually printed on the first page of the exam booklet. As a rule, these instructions refer to the timing of the examination; the fact that you should not start work until the signal and must stop work at a signal, etc. If there are any *special* instructions, such as a choice of questions to be answered, make sure that you note this instruction carefully.

2) When you are ready to start work on the examination, that is as soon as the signal has been given, read the instructions to each question booklet, underline any key words or phrases, such as *least, best, outline, describe* and the like. In this way you will tend to answer as requested rather than discover on reviewing your paper that you *listed without describing*, that you selected the *worst* choice rather than the *best* choice, etc.

3) If the examination is of the objective or multiple-choice type – that is, each question will also give a series of possible answers: A, B, C or D, and you are called upon to select the best answer and write the letter next to that answer on your answer paper – it is advisable to start answering each question in turn. There may be anywhere from 50 to 100 such questions in the three or four hours allotted and you can see how much time would be taken if you read through all the questions before beginning to answer any. Furthermore, if you come across a question or group of questions which you know would be difficult to answer, it would undoubtedly affect your handling of all the other questions.

4) If the examination is of the essay type and contains but a few questions, it is a moot point as to whether you should read all the questions before starting to answer any one. Of course, if you are given a choice – say five out of seven and the like – then it is essential to read all the questions so you can eliminate the two that are most difficult. If, however, you are asked to answer all the questions, there may be danger in trying to answer the easiest one first because you may find that you will spend too much time on it. The best technique is to answer the first question, then proceed to the second, etc.

5) Time your answers. Before the exam begins, write down the time it started, then add the time allowed for the examination and write down the time it must be completed, then divide the time available somewhat as follows:
    - If 3-1/2 hours are allowed, that would be 210 minutes. If you have 80 objective-type questions, that would be an average of 2-1/2 minutes per question. Allow yourself no more than 2 minutes per question, or a total of 160 minutes, which will permit about 50 minutes to review.
    - If for the time allotment of 210 minutes there are 7 essay questions to answer, that would average about 30 minutes a question. Give yourself only 25 minutes per question so that you have about 35 minutes to review.

6) The most important instruction is to *read each question* and make sure you know what is wanted. The second most important instruction is to *time yourself properly* so that you answer every question. The third most important instruction is to *answer every question*. Guess if you have to but include something for each question. Remember that you will receive no credit for a blank and will probably receive some credit if you write something in answer to an essay question. If you guess a letter – say "B" for a multiple-choice question – you may have guessed right. If you leave a blank as an answer to a multiple-choice question, the examiners may respect your feelings but it will not add a point to your score. Some exams may penalize you for wrong answers, so in such cases *only*, you may not want to guess unless you have some basis for your answer.

7) Suggestions
    a. Objective-type questions
        1. Examine the question booklet for proper sequence of pages and questions
        2. Read all instructions carefully
        3. Skip any question which seems too difficult; return to it after all other questions have been answered
        4. Apportion your time properly; do not spend too much time on any single question or group of questions

5. Note and underline key words – *all, most, fewest, least, best, worst, same, opposite,* etc.
6. Pay particular attention to negatives
7. Note unusual option, e.g., unduly long, short, complex, different or similar in content to the body of the question
8. Observe the use of "hedging" words – *probably, may, most likely,* etc.
9. Make sure that your answer is put next to the same number as the question
10. Do not second-guess unless you have good reason to believe the second answer is definitely more correct
11. Cross out original answer if you decide another answer is more accurate; do not erase until you are ready to hand your paper in
12. Answer all questions; guess unless instructed otherwise
13. Leave time for review

   b. Essay questions
   1. Read each question carefully
   2. Determine exactly what is wanted. Underline key words or phrases.
   3. Decide on outline or paragraph answer
   4. Include many different points and elements unless asked to develop any one or two points or elements
   5. Show impartiality by giving pros and cons unless directed to select one side only
   6. Make and write down any assumptions you find necessary to answer the questions
   7. Watch your English, grammar, punctuation and choice of words
   8. Time your answers; don't crowd material

8) Answering the essay question

Most essay questions can be answered by framing the specific response around several key words or ideas. Here are a few such key words or ideas:

M's: manpower, materials, methods, money, management
P's: purpose, program, policy, plan, procedure, practice, problems, pitfalls, personnel, public relations

   a. Six basic steps in handling problems:
   1. Preliminary plan and background development
   2. Collect information, data and facts
   3. Analyze and interpret information, data and facts
   4. Analyze and develop solutions as well as make recommendations
   5. Prepare report and sell recommendations
   6. Install recommendations and follow up effectiveness

   b. Pitfalls to avoid
   1. *Taking things for granted* – A statement of the situation does not necessarily imply that each of the elements is necessarily true; for example, a complaint may be invalid and biased so that all that can be taken for granted is that a complaint has been registered

2. *Considering only one side of a situation* – Wherever possible, indicate several alternatives and then point out the reasons you selected the best one
3. *Failing to indicate follow up* – Whenever your answer indicates action on your part, make certain that you will take proper follow-up action to see how successful your recommendations, procedures or actions turn out to be
4. *Taking too long in answering any single question* – Remember to time your answers properly

IX. AFTER THE TEST

Scoring procedures differ in detail among civil service jurisdictions although the general principles are the same. Whether the papers are hand-scored or graded by machine we have described, they are nearly always graded by number. That is, the person who marks the paper knows only the number – never the name – of the applicant. Not until all the papers have been graded will they be matched with names. If other tests, such as training and experience or oral interview ratings have been given, scores will be combined. Different parts of the examination usually have different weights. For example, the written test might count 60 percent of the final grade, and a rating of training and experience 40 percent. In many jurisdictions, veterans will have a certain number of points added to their grades.

After the final grade has been determined, the names are placed in grade order and an eligible list is established. There are various methods for resolving ties between those who get the same final grade – probably the most common is to place first the name of the person whose application was received first. Job offers are made from the eligible list in the order the names appear on it. You will be notified of your grade and your rank as soon as all these computations have been made. This will be done as rapidly as possible.

People who are found to meet the requirements in the announcement are called "eligibles." Their names are put on a list of eligible candidates. An eligible's chances of getting a job depend on how high he stands on this list and how fast agencies are filling jobs from the list.

When a job is to be filled from a list of eligibles, the agency asks for the names of people on the list of eligibles for that job. When the civil service commission receives this request, it sends to the agency the names of the three people highest on this list. Or, if the job to be filled has specialized requirements, the office sends the agency the names of the top three persons who meet these requirements from the general list.

The appointing officer makes a choice from among the three people whose names were sent to him. If the selected person accepts the appointment, the names of the others are put back on the list to be considered for future openings.

That is the rule in hiring from all kinds of eligible lists, whether they are for typist, carpenter, chemist, or something else. For every vacancy, the appointing officer has his choice of any one of the top three eligibles on the list. This explains why the person whose name is on top of the list sometimes does not get an appointment when some of the persons lower on the list do. If the appointing officer chooses the second or third eligible, the No. 1 eligible does not get a job at once, but stays on the list until he is appointed or the list is terminated.

X. HOW TO PASS THE INTERVIEW TEST

The examination for which you applied requires an oral interview test. You have already taken the written test and you are now being called for the interview test – the final part of the formal examination.

You may think that it is not possible to prepare for an interview test and that there are no procedures to follow during an interview. Our purpose is to point out some things you can do in advance that will help you and some good rules to follow and pitfalls to avoid while you are being interviewed.

What is an interview supposed to test?

The written examination is designed to test the technical knowledge and competence of the candidate; the oral is designed to evaluate intangible qualities, not readily measured otherwise, and to establish a list showing the relative fitness of each candidate – as measured against his competitors – for the position sought. Scoring is not on the basis of "right" and "wrong," but on a sliding scale of values ranging from "not passable" to "outstanding." As a matter of fact, it is possible to achieve a relatively low score without a single "incorrect" answer because of evident weakness in the qualities being measured.

Occasionally, an examination may consist entirely of an oral test – either an individual or a group oral. In such cases, information is sought concerning the technical knowledges and abilities of the candidate, since there has been no written examination for this purpose. More commonly, however, an oral test is used to supplement a written examination.

Who conducts interviews?

The composition of oral boards varies among different jurisdictions. In nearly all, a representative of the personnel department serves as chairman. One of the members of the board may be a representative of the department in which the candidate would work. In some cases, "outside experts" are used, and, frequently, a businessman or some other representative of the general public is asked to serve. Labor and management or other special groups may be represented. The aim is to secure the services of experts in the appropriate field.

However the board is composed, it is a good idea (and not at all improper or unethical) to ascertain in advance of the interview who the members are and what groups they represent. When you are introduced to them, you will have some idea of their backgrounds and interests, and at least you will not stutter and stammer over their names.

What should be done before the interview?

While knowledge about the board members is useful and takes some of the surprise element out of the interview, there is other preparation which is more substantive. It *is* possible to prepare for an oral interview – in several ways:

1) Keep a copy of your application and review it carefully before the interview

This may be the only document before the oral board, and the starting point of the interview. Know what education and experience you have listed there, and the sequence and dates of all of it. Sometimes the board will ask you to review the highlights of your experience for them; you should not have to hem and haw doing it.

2) Study the class specification and the examination announcement

Usually, the oral board has one or both of these to guide them. The qualities, characteristics or knowledges required by the position sought are stated in these documents. They offer valuable clues as to the nature of the oral interview. For example, if the job involves supervisory responsibilities, the announcement will usually indicate that knowledge of modern supervisory methods and the qualifications of the candidate as a supervisor will be tested. If so, you can expect such questions, frequently in the form of a hypothetical situation which you are expected to solve. NEVER go into an oral without knowledge of the duties and responsibilities of the job you seek.

3) Think through each qualification required

Try to visualize the kind of questions you would ask if you were a board member. How well could you answer them? Try especially to appraise your own knowledge and background in each area, *measured against the job sought*, and identify any areas in which you are weak. Be critical and realistic – do not flatter yourself.

4) Do some general reading in areas in which you feel you may be weak

For example, if the job involves supervision and your past experience has NOT, some general reading in supervisory methods and practices, particularly in the field of human relations, might be useful. Do NOT study agency procedures or detailed manuals. The oral board will be testing your understanding and capacity, not your memory.

5) Get a good night's sleep and watch your general health and mental attitude

You will want a clear head at the interview. Take care of a cold or any other minor ailment, and of course, no hangovers.

What should be done on the day of the interview?

Now comes the day of the interview itself. Give yourself plenty of time to get there. Plan to arrive somewhat ahead of the scheduled time, particularly if your appointment is in the fore part of the day. If a previous candidate fails to appear, the board might be ready for you a bit early. By early afternoon an oral board is almost invariably behind schedule if there are many candidates, and you may have to wait. Take along a book or magazine to read, or your application to review, but leave any extraneous material in the waiting room when you go in for your interview. In any event, relax and compose yourself.

The matter of dress is important. The board is forming impressions about you – from your experience, your manners, your attitude, and your appearance. Give your personal appearance careful attention. Dress your best, but not your flashiest. Choose conservative, appropriate clothing, and be sure it is immaculate. This is a business interview, and your appearance should indicate that you regard it as such. Besides, being well groomed and properly dressed will help boost your confidence.

Sooner or later, someone will call your name and escort you into the interview room. *This is it.* From here on you are on your own. It is too late for any more preparation. But remember, you asked for this opportunity to prove your fitness, and you are here because your request was granted.

What happens when you go in?

The usual sequence of events will be as follows: The clerk (who is often the board stenographer) will introduce you to the chairman of the oral board, who will introduce you to the other members of the board. Acknowledge the introductions before you sit down. Do not be surprised if you find a microphone facing you or a stenotypist sitting by. Oral interviews are usually recorded in the event of an appeal or other review.

Usually the chairman of the board will open the interview by reviewing the highlights of your education and work experience from your application – primarily for the benefit of the other members of the board, as well as to get the material into the record. Do not interrupt or comment unless there is an error or significant misinterpretation; if that is the case, do not hesitate. But do not quibble about insignificant matters. Also, he will usually ask you some question about your education, experience or your present job – partly to get you to start talking and to establish the interviewing "rapport." He may start the actual questioning, or turn it over to one of the other members. Frequently, each member undertakes the questioning on a particular area, one in which he is perhaps most competent, so you can expect each member to participate in the examination. Because time is limited, you may also expect some rather abrupt switches in the direction the questioning takes, so do not be upset by it. Normally, a board member will not pursue a single line of questioning unless he discovers a particular strength or weakness.

After each member has participated, the chairman will usually ask whether any member has any further questions, then will ask you if you have anything you wish to add. Unless you are expecting this question, it may floor you. Worse, it may start you off on an extended, extemporaneous speech. The board is not usually seeking more information. The question is principally to offer you a last opportunity to present further qualifications or to indicate that you have nothing to add. So, if you feel that a significant qualification or characteristic has been overlooked, it is proper to point it out in a sentence or so. Do not compliment the board on the thoroughness of their examination – they have been sketchy, and you know it. If you wish, merely say, "No thank you, I have nothing further to add." This is a point where you can "talk yourself out" of a good impression or fail to present an important bit of information. Remember, *you close the interview yourself*.

The chairman will then say, "That is all, Mr. _____, thank you." Do not be startled; the interview is over, and quicker than you think. Thank him, gather your belongings and take your leave. Save your sigh of relief for the other side of the door.

How to put your best foot forward

Throughout this entire process, you may feel that the board individually and collectively is trying to pierce your defenses, seek out your hidden weaknesses and embarrass and confuse you. Actually, this is not true. They are obliged to make an appraisal of your qualifications for the job you are seeking, and they want to see you in your best light. Remember, they must interview all candidates and a non-cooperative candidate may become a failure in spite of their best efforts to bring out his qualifications. Here are 15 suggestions that will help you:

1) Be natural – Keep your attitude confident, not cocky

If you are not confident that you can do the job, do not expect the board to be. Do not apologize for your weaknesses, try to bring out your strong points. The board is interested in a positive, not negative, presentation. Cockiness will antagonize any board member and make him wonder if you are covering up a weakness by a false show of strength.

2) Get comfortable, but don't lounge or sprawl

Sit erectly but not stiffly. A careless posture may lead the board to conclude that you are careless in other things, or at least that you are not impressed by the importance of the occasion. Either conclusion is natural, even if incorrect. Do not fuss with your clothing, a pencil or an ashtray. Your hands may occasionally be useful to emphasize a point; do not let them become a point of distraction.

3) Do not wisecrack or make small talk

This is a serious situation, and your attitude should show that you consider it as such. Further, the time of the board is limited – they do not want to waste it, and neither should you.

4) Do not exaggerate your experience or abilities

In the first place, from information in the application or other interviews and sources, the board may know more about you than you think. Secondly, you probably will not get away with it. An experienced board is rather adept at spotting such a situation, so do not take the chance.

5) If you know a board member, do not make a point of it, yet do not hide it

Certainly you are not fooling him, and probably not the other members of the board. Do not try to take advantage of your acquaintanceship – it will probably do you little good.

6) Do not dominate the interview

Let the board do that. They will give you the clues – do not assume that you have to do all the talking. Realize that the board has a number of questions to ask you, and do not try to take up all the interview time by showing off your extensive knowledge of the answer to the first one.

7) Be attentive

You only have 20 minutes or so, and you should keep your attention at its sharpest throughout. When a member is addressing a problem or question to you, give him your undivided attention. Address your reply principally to him, but do not exclude the other board members.

8) Do not interrupt

A board member may be stating a problem for you to analyze. He will ask you a question when the time comes. Let him state the problem, and wait for the question.

9) Make sure you understand the question

Do not try to answer until you are sure what the question is. If it is not clear, restate it in your own words or ask the board member to clarify it for you. However, do not haggle about minor elements.

10) Reply promptly but not hastily

A common entry on oral board rating sheets is "candidate responded readily," or "candidate hesitated in replies." Respond as promptly and quickly as you can, but do not jump to a hasty, ill-considered answer.

11) Do not be peremptory in your answers

A brief answer is proper – but do not fire your answer back. That is a losing game from your point of view. The board member can probably ask questions much faster than you can answer them.

12) Do not try to create the answer you think the board member wants

He is interested in what kind of mind you have and how it works – not in playing games. Furthermore, he can usually spot this practice and will actually grade you down on it.

13) Do not switch sides in your reply merely to agree with a board member

Frequently, a member will take a contrary position merely to draw you out and to see if you are willing and able to defend your point of view. Do not start a debate, yet do not surrender a good position. If a position is worth taking, it is worth defending.

14) Do not be afraid to admit an error in judgment if you are shown to be wrong

The board knows that you are forced to reply without any opportunity for careful consideration. Your answer may be demonstrably wrong. If so, admit it and get on with the interview.

15) Do not dwell at length on your present job

The opening question may relate to your present assignment. Answer the question but do not go into an extended discussion. You are being examined for a *new* job, not your present one. As a matter of fact, try to phrase ALL your answers in terms of the job for which you are being examined.

Basis of Rating

Probably you will forget most of these "do's" and "don'ts" when you walk into the oral interview room. Even remembering them all will not ensure you a passing grade. Perhaps you did not have the qualifications in the first place. But remembering them will help you to put your best foot forward, without treading on the toes of the board members.

Rumor and popular opinion to the contrary notwithstanding, an oral board wants you to make the best appearance possible. They know you are under pressure – but they also want to see how you respond to it as a guide to what your reaction would be under the pressures of the job you seek. They will be influenced by the degree of poise you display, the personal traits you show and the manner in which you respond.

ABOUT THIS BOOK

This book contains tests divided into Examination Sections. Go through each test, answering every question in the margin. We have also attached a sample answer sheet at the back of the book that can be removed and used. At the end of each test look at the answer key and check your answers. On the ones you got wrong, look at the right answer choice and learn. Do not fill in the answers first. Do not memorize the questions and answers, but understand the answer and principles involved. On your test, the questions will likely be different from the samples. Questions are changed and new ones added. If you understand these past questions you should have success with any changes that arise. Tests may consist of several types of questions. We have additional books on each subject should more study be advisable or necessary for you. Finally, the more you study, the better prepared you will be. This book is intended to be the last thing you study before you walk into the examination room. Prior study of relevant texts is also recommended. NLC publishes some of these in our Fundamental Series. Knowledge and good sense are important factors in passing your exam. Good luck also helps. So now study this Passbook, absorb the material contained within and take that knowledge into the examination. Then do your best to pass that exam.

EXAMINATION SECTION

EXAMINATION SECTION
TEST 1

DIRECTIONS: Each question or incomplete statement is followed by several suggested answers or completions. Select the one that BEST answers the question or completes the statement. *PRINT THE LETTER OF THE CORRECT ANSWER IN THE SPACE AT THE RIGHT.*

1. Which of the following is the LEAST important factor to consider in surveying the physical layout of a building for traffic flow?

   A. Location of windows
   B. Number of entrances
   C. Number of exits
   D. Location of first aid rooms

2. The major purpose of any security program in a large organization is to prevent unlawful acts.
   If adequate patrol coverage is provided at a given location, it is MOST likely that

   A. crimes will not be committed
   B. undesirables will not enter the building
   C. unlawful acts will increase in the long run
   D. there will be less opportunity to commit a crime

3. The MOST frequent cause of fires in public facilities is

   A. incinerators   B. vandalism
   C. electrical sources D. smoking on the job

4. After bomb threats are received, it is sometimes necessary to evacuate a facility. How long BEFORE the threatened time of explosion should a facility be evacuated?
   At least _____ minutes.

   A. 15   B. 25   C. 50   D. 60

5. Once a facility is evacuated because of a bomb threat, how much time should pass before the public and employees are allowed to enter the building?
   _____ minutes.

   A. 10   B. 20   C. 40   D. 60

6. Of the following locations in public buildings, the one which is the LEAST likely place for bombs to be planted is in

   A. storerooms   B. bathrooms
   C. cafeterias   D. waste receptacles

7. The one of the following that is the surest means of establishing positive identification of someone entering a facility is by

   A. personal recognition   B. I.D. badge
   C. social security card   D. driver's license

8. The one of the following which most probably would NOT be included in a police record report concerning an incident at a facility is the

   A. name of complainant or injured party
   B. name of the investigating officer
   C. statement of each witness
   D. religion of complainant or injured party

9. Preventing trouble is one of the primary concerns of special officers.
   When dealing with unruly groups of people who threaten to become violent, which of the following is a measure which should NOT be taken?

   A. Maintain close surveillance of such groups
   B. Try to contact the leaders of the group regardless of their militancy
   C. Keep the officer force alerted
   D. Have the officer force deal aggressively with provocations

10. Of the following, the MOST important factor to consider in the deployment of officers dealing with a client population is the officers' ability to

    A. remain calm
    B. look stern
    C. evaluate personality
    D. take a firm stand

11. Assume that an offender is struggling with a group of officers who are trying to arrest him.
    What force, if any, can be used to overcome this resistance?

    A. The amount of force acceptable to the public
    B. The amount of force necessary to restrain the offender and protect the officers
    C. Any amount of force that is acceptable to the officers at the scene
    D. No force may be used until the police arrive

12. Assume that a fire is discovered at your work location. The one of the following actions which would be INAPPROPRIATE for you to take is to

    A. notify the telephone operator
    B. station a reliable person at the entrance
    C. open all windows and doors in the area
    D. start evacuating the area

13. If a person has an object caught in his throat or air passage but is breathing adequately, which one of the following should you do?

    A. Probe for the object
    B. Force him to drink water
    C. Lay him over your arm and slap him between the shoulder blades
    D. Allow him to cough and to assume the position he finds most comfortable

14. The one of the following methods which should NOT be used to report a fire is to

    A. call 911
    B. pull the handle in the red box on the street corner
    C. call the fire department county numbers listed in each county directory
    D. call 411

15. Assume that an officer, alone in a building at night, smells the strong odor of cooking or heating gas. In addition to airing the building and making sure that he is not overcome, it would be BEST for the officer to call

   A. his superior at his home and ask for instructions
   B. for a plumber from the department of public works
   C. 911 for police and fire help
   D. the emergency number at Con Edison

16. Of the following situations, the one that is MOST dangerous for an officer is when he

   A. investigates suspicious persons and circumstances
   B. finds a burglary in progress or pursues burglary suspects
   C. attempts an arrest or finds a robbery in progress
   D. patrols on the overnight shift

17. An officer on security patrol generally should spend MOST of his time

   A. checking doors and locks
   B. helping the public and answering questions
   C. chasing criminals and looking for clues
   D. writing reports on unusual incidents

18. The one of the following that is an ACCEPTABLE way to arrest a person is to

   A. tell him to report to the nearest police precinct
   B. send a summons to his permanent address
   C. tell him in person that he is under arrest
   D. show him handcuffs and ask him to come along

19. A carbon dioxide fire extinguisher is BEST suited for extinguishing _____ fires.

   A. paper   B. rag   C. rubbish   D. grease

20. A pressurized water or soda-acid fire extinguisher is BEST suited for extinguishing _____ fires.

   A. wood   B. gasoline
   C. electrical   D. magnesium

21. The one of the following statements that does NOT apply to the use of handcuffs is that they

   A. are used as temporary restraining devices
   B. eliminate the need for vigilance
   C. cannot be opened without keys
   D. are used to secure a violent person

22. The one of the following that is GENERALLY a crime against the person is

   A. trespass   B. burglary   C. robbery   D. arson

23. Of the following, the SAFEST way of escape from an office in a burning building is generally the

    A. stairway
    B. rooftop
    C. passenger elevator
    D. freight elevator

24. In attempting to control a possible riot situation, an officer pushed his way into a crowd gathered outside the building and tried to cause confusion by arguing with members of the group.
    This procedure NORMALLY is considered

    A. *desirable;* any violence that occurs will remain outside the building
    B. *desirable;* the crowd will break into smaller groups and disperse
    C. *undesirable;* to maintain control of the situation, the officer must not become part of the crowd
    D. *undesirable;* the supervisor should stay clear of the scene

25. Which one of the following is MOST effective in making officers more safety-minded?

    A. Maintaining an up-to-date library of the latest safety literature
    B. Reading daily safety bulletins at roll-call
    C. Holding informal group safety meetings periodically
    D. Offering prizes for good safety slogans and displays

KEY (CORRECT ANSWERS)

1.	A	11.	B
2.	D	12.	C
3.	C	13.	D
4.	A	14.	D
5.	D	15.	D
6.	C	16.	C
7.	A	17.	A
8.	D	18.	C
9.	D	19.	D
10.	A	20.	A

21.	B
22.	C
23.	A
24.	C
25.	C

TEST 2

DIRECTIONS: Each question or incomplete statement is followed by several suggested answers or completions. Select the one that BEST answers the question or completes the statement. *PRINT THE LETTER OF THE CORRECT ANSWER IN THE SPACE AT THE RIGHT.*

1. Assume that an angry crowd of some 75 to 100 people has built up in one of the hallways of a center and that only one superior officer and two subordinate officers are on duty in the building. A glass panel in one of the stairway doors has just been broken under the pressure of the crowd and a bench has been hurled down a flight of stairs. The one of the following actions that the superior officer SHOULD take in this situation is to

    A. push his way into the crowd and try to reason with them
    B. order the two other officers to try to quiet the crowd
    C. call the police on 911 and meet them outside the building
    D. do nothing at this point in order to avoid a riot

    1._____

2. One of the duties and responsibilities of a supervisor is to test the knowledge of the officers concerning their post conditions.
   This should be done if the officer's assignment is

    A. fixed only
    B. roving only
    C. roving only in a troublesome spot
    D. either fixed or roving

    2._____

3. An officer discovers early one morning that an office in the building he guards has been burglarized.
   Of the following, it is important for the officer to FIRST

    A. go through the building and look for suspects
    B. call the police and protect the area and whatever evidence exists until they arrive
    C. allow people into their offices as they come to work
    D. examine, sort, and handle all evidence before the police get there

    3._____

4. Assume that two officers are interrogating one suspect. How should these officers position themselves during the interrogation?

    A. One officer should stand on either side of the suspect.
    B. One officer should stand to the right of the suspect, and the other officer should stand behind the suspect.
    C. Both officers should stand to the right of the suspect.
    D. One officer should stand to the right of the suspect, and the other officer should stand in front of the suspect.

    4._____

5. A witness who takes an oath to testify truly and who states as true any matter which he knows to be false is guilty of

    A. perjury   B. libel   C. slander   D. fraud

    5._____

6. An officer checking a substance suspected of containing narcotics should GENERALLY

   A. taste it in small amounts
   B. send it to a laboratory for analysis
   C. smell it for its distinctive odor
   D. examine it for its unusual texture

7. A certain center is situated in an area where frequent outbreaks of hostilities seem to be focused on the center itself.
   Which of the following BEST explains why the center may be a target for hostile acts?
   It

   A. serves community needs
   B. represents governmental authority
   C. represents all ethnic groups
   D. serves as a neutral battlefield

8. An officer often deals with people who might be addicted to drugs.
   The one of the following symptoms which is NOT generally an indication of drug addiction is

   A. dilation of the eye pupils
   B. frequent yawning and sneezing
   C. a deep, rasping cough
   D. continual itching of the arms and legs

9. In emergency situations, panic will MOST probably occur when people are

   A. unexpectedly confronted with a terrorizing condition from which there appears to be no escape
   B. angry and violent
   C. anxious about circumstances which are not obvious, easily visible or within the immediate area
   D. familiar with the effects of the emergency

10. The one of the following actions on the part of a person that would NOT be considered *resisting arrest* is

    A. retreating and running away
    B. saying, *You can't arrest me*
    C. pushing the officer aside
    D. pulling away from an officer's grasp

11. Which of the following items would NOT be considered an APPROPRIATE item of uniform for an officer to wear while on duty?

    A. Reefer type overcoat
    B. Leather laced shoes with flat soles
    C. White socks
    D. Cap cover with cap device displayed

12. What can happen to an officer if the leather thong on his night stick is NOT twisted correctly?
    The

    A. baton may be taken out of the officer's hand
    B. officer's wrist may be broken
    C. leather will tear more easily
    D. officer's arm may be injured

13. The one of the following kinds of information which SHOULD be included in the log book is

    A. any important matter of police information
    B. an item noted in Standard Operating Procedures only
    C. everything of general interest
    D. a crime or offense only

14. While on patrol at your work location, you receive a call that an assault has taken place. Upon your arrival at the scene, the victim, who has severe lacerations, informs you that the assailant ran into a nearby basement.
    After apprehending the suspect, the type of search you should conduct is a _____ search.

    A. wall   B. frisk   C. body   D. strip

15. A tactical force is valuable in MOST emergency situations PRIMARILY because of its

    A. location   B. morale
    C. flexibility   D. size

16. An officer should be encouraged to talk easily and frankly when he is dealing with his superior.
    In order to encourage such free communication, it would be MOST appropriate for a superior to behave in a(n)

    A. *sincere* manner; assure the officer that you will deal with him honestly and openly
    B. *official* manner; you are a superior officer and must always act formally with subordinates
    C. *investigative* manner; you must probe and question to get to a basis of trust
    D. *unemotional* manner; the officer's emotions and background should play no part in your dealings with him

17. Research findings show that an increase in free communication within an agency GENERALLY results in which one of the following?

    A. Improved morale and productivity
    B. Increased promotional opportunities
    C. An increase in authority
    D. A spirit of honesty

18. Assume that you are a superior officer and your superiors have given you a new arrest procedure to be followed. Before passing this information on to your subordinates, the one of the following actions that you should take FIRST is to

    A. ask your superiors to send out a memorandum to the entire staff
    B. clarify the procedure in your own mind
    C. set up a training course to provide instructions on the new procedure
    D. write a memorandum to your subordinates

19. Communication is necessary for an organization to be effective.
    The one of the following which is LEAST important for most communication systems is that

    A. messages are sent quickly and directly to the person who needs them to operate
    B. information should be conveyed understandably and accurately
    C. the method used to transmit information should be kept secret so that security can be maintained
    D. senders of messages must know how their messages were received and acted upon

20. Which one of the following is the CHIEF advantage of listening willingly to subordinate officers and encouraging them to talk freely and honestly?
    It

    A. reveals to superiors the degree to which ideas that are passed down are accepted by subordinates
    B. reduces the participation of subordinates in the operation of the department
    C. encourages officers to try for promotion
    D. enables officers to learn about security leaks on the part of officials

21. A superior may be informed through either oral or written reports.
    Which one of the following is an ADVANTAGE of using oral reports?

    A. There is no need for a formal record of the report.
    B. An exact duplicate of the report is not easily transmitted to others.
    C. A good oral report requires little time for preparation.
    D. An oral report involves two-way communication between a subordinate and his superior.

22. Of the following, the MOST important reason why officers should communicate effectively with the public is to

    A. improve the public's understanding of information that is important for them to know
    B. establish a friendly relationship
    C. obtain information about the kinds of people who come to the center
    D. convince the public that services are adequate

23. Officers should generally NOT use phrases like *too hard, too easy,* and *a lot* principally because such phrases

    A. may be offensive to some minority groups
    B. are too informal

C. mean different things to different people
D. are difficult to remember

24. The ability to communicate clearly and concisely is an important element in effective leadership.
Which of the following statements about oral and written communication is GENERALLY true?

A. Oral communication is more time-consuming.
B. Written communication is more likely to be misinterpreted.
C. Oral communication is useful only in emergencies.
D. Written communication is useful mainly when giving information to fewer than twenty people.

25. Rumors can often have harmful and disruptive effects on an organization.
Which one of the following is the BEST way to prevent rumors from becoming a problem?

A. Refuse to act on rumors, thereby making them less believable
B. Increase the amount of information passed along by the *grapevine*
C. Distribute as much factual information as possible
D. Provide training in report writing

KEY (CORRECT ANSWERS)

1. C		11. C	
2. D		12. A	
3. B		13. A	
4. B		14. A	
5. A		15. C	
6. B		16. A	
7. B		17. A	
8. C		18. B	
9. A		19. C	
10. B		20. A	

21. D
22. A
23. C
24. B
25. C

EXAMINATION SECTION
TEST 1

DIRECTIONS: Each question or incomplete statement is followed by several suggested answers or completions. Select the one that BEST answers the question or completes the statement. *PRINT THE LETTER OF THE CORRECT ANSWER IN THE SPACE AT THE RIGHT.*

1. The officer who investigates accidents is always required to make a complete and accurate report.
   Of the following, the BEST reason for this procedure is to

   A. protect the operating agency against possible false claims
   B. provide a file of incidents which can be used as basic material for an accident prevention campaign
   C. provide the management with concrete evidence of violations of the rules by employees
   D. indicate what repairs need to be made

2. It is suggested that an officer keep all persons away from the area of an accident until an investigation has been completed.
   This suggested procedure is

   A. *good;* witnesses will be more likely to agree on a single story
   B. *bad;* such action blocks traffic flow and causes congestion
   C. *good;* objects of possible use as evidence will be protected from damage or loss
   D. *bad;* the flow of normal pedestrian traffic provides an opportunity for an investigator to determine the cause of the accident

3. A man having business with your agency is arguing with you and accuses you of being prejudiced against him. Although you explain to him that this is not so, he demands to see your supervisor.
   Of the following, the BEST course of action for you to take is to

   A. continue arguing with him until you have worn him out or convinced him
   B. take him to your supervisor
   C. ignore him and walk away from him to another part of the office
   D. escort him out of the office

4. An officer receives instructions from his supervisor which he does not fully understand.
   For the officer to ask for a further explanation would be

   A. *good;* chiefly because his supervisor will be impressed with his interest in his work
   B. *poor;* chiefly because the time of the supervisor will be needlessly wasted
   C. *good;* chiefly because proper performance depends on full understanding of the work to be done
   D. *poor;* chiefly because officers should be able to think for themselves

5. A person is making a complaint to an officer which seems unreasonable and of little importance.
   Of the following, the BEST action for the officer to take is to

A. criticize the person making the complaint for taking up his valuable time
B. laugh over the matter to show that the complaint is minor and silly
C. tell the person that anyone responsible for his grievance will be prosecuted
D. listen to the person making the complaint and tell him that the matter will be investigated

6. A member of the department shall not indulge in intoxicating liquor while in uniform. A member of the department is not required to wear a uniform, and a uniformed member while out of uniform shall not indulge in intoxicants to an extent unfitting him for duty.
Of the following, the MOST correct interpretation of this rule is that a

   A. member, off duty, not in uniform, may drink intoxicating liquor
   B. member, not on duty, but in uniform, may drink intoxicating liquor
   C. member, on duty, in uniform, may drink intoxicants
   D. uniformed member, in civilian clothes, may not drink intoxicants

7. You have a suggestion for an important change which you believe will improve a certain procedure in your agency. Of the following, the next course of action for you to take is to

   A. try it out yourself
   B. submit the suggestion to your immediate supervisor
   C. write a letter to the head of your agency asking for his approval
   D. wait until you are asked for suggestions before submitting this one

8. An officer shall study maps and literature concerning his assigned area and the streets and points of interest nearby.
Of the following, the BEST reason for this rule is that

   A. the officer will be better able to give correct information to persons desiring it
   B. the officer will be better able to drive a vehicle in the area
   C. the officer will not lose interest in his work
   D. supervisors will not need to train the officers in this subject

9. In asking a witness to a crime to identify a suspect, it is a common practice to place the suspect with a group of persons and ask the witness to pick out the person in question.
Of the following, the BEST reason for this practice is that it will

   A. make the identification more reliable than if the witness were shown the suspect alone
   B. protect the witness against reprisals
   C. make sure that the witness is telling the truth
   D. help select other participants in the crime at the same time

10. It is most important for all officers to obey the "Rules and Regulations" of their agency.
Of the following, the BEST reason for this statement is that

    A. supervisors will not need to train their new officers
    B. officers will never have to use their own judgment
    C. uniform procedures will be followed
    D. officers will not need to ask their supervisors for assistance

Questions 11-13.

DIRECTIONS: Answer questions 11 to 13 SOLELY on the basis of the following paragraph.

All members of the police force must recognize that the people, through their representatives, hire and pay the police and that, as in any other employment, there must exist a proper employer-employee relationship. The police officer must understand that the essence of a correct police attitude is a willingness to serve, but at the same time, he should distinguish between service and servility, and between courtesy and softness. He must be firm but also courteous, avoiding even an appearance of rudeness. He should develop a position that is friendly and unbiased, pleasant and sympathetic, in his relations with the general public, but firm and impersonal on occasions calling for regulation and control. A police officer should understand that his primary purpose is to prevent violations, not to arrest people. He should recognize the line of demarcation between a police function and passing judgment which is a court function. On the other side, a public that cooperates with the police, that supports them in their efforts and that observes laws and regulations, may be said to have a desirable attitude.

11. In accordance with this paragraph, the PROPER attitude for a police officer to take is to   11.____

    A. be pleasant and sympathetic at all times
    B. be friendly, firm, and impartial
    C. be stern and severe in meting out justice to all
    D. avoid being rude, except in those cases where the public is uncooperative

12. Assume that an officer is assigned by his superior officer to a busy traffic intersection and   12.____
    is warned to be on the lookout for motorists who skip the light or who are speeding.
    According to this paragraph, it would be proper for the officer in this assignment to

    A. give a summons to every motorist whose ear was crossing when the light changed
    B. hide behind a truck and wait for drivers who violate traffic laws
    C. select at random motorists who seem to be impatient and lecture them sternly on traffic safety
    D. stand on post in order to deter violations and give offenders a summons or a warning as required

13. According to this paragraph, a police officer must realize that the primary purpose of   13.____
    police work is to

    A. provide proper police service in a courteous manner
    B. decide whether those who violate the law should be punished
    C. arrest those who violate laws
    D. establish a proper employer-employee relationship

Questions 14-15.

DIRECTIONS: Answer questions 14 and 15 SOLELY on the basis of the following paragraph.

If a motor vehicle fails to pass inspection, the owner will be given a rejection notice by the inspection station. Repairs must be made within ten days after this notice is issued. It is not necessary to have the required adjustment or repairs made at the station where the inspection occurred. The vehicle may be taken to any other garage. Re-inspection after repairs may be made at any official inspection station, not necessarily the same station which made the initial inspection. The registration of any motor vehicle for which an inspection sticker has not been obtained as required, or which is not repaired and inspected within ten days after inspection indicates defects, is subject to suspension. A vehicle cannot be used on public highways while its registration is under suspension.

14. According to the above paragraph, the owner of a car which does NOT pass inspection must

    A. have repairs made at the same station which rejected his car
    B. take the car to another station and have it re-inspected
    C. have repairs made anywhere and then have the car re-inspected
    D. not use the car on a public highway until the necessary repairs have been made

15. According to the above paragraph, the one of the following which may be cause for suspension of the registration of a vehicle is that

    A. an inspection sticker was issued before the rejection notice had been in force for ten days
    B. it was not re-inspected by the station that rejected it originally
    C. it was not re-inspected either by the station that rejected it originally or by the garage which made the repairs
    D. it has not had defective parts repaired within ten days after inspection

Questions 16-20.

DIRECTIONS: Answer questions 16 to 20 SOLELY on the basis of the following paragraph.

If we are to study crime in its widest social setting, we will find a variety of conduct which, although criminal in the legal sense, is not offensive to the moral conscience of a considerable number of persons. Traffic violations, for example, do not brand the offender as guilty of moral offense. In fact, the recipient of a traffic ticket is usually simply the subject of some good-natured joking by his friends. Although there may be indignation among certain groups of citizens against gambling and liquor law violations, these activities are often tolerated, if not openly supported, by the more numerous residents of the community. Indeed, certain social and service clubs regularly conduct gambling games and lotteries for the purpose of raising funds. Some communities regard violations involving the sale of liquor with little concern in order to profit from increased license fees and taxes paid by dealers. The thousand and one forms of political graft and corruption which infest our urban centers only occasionally arouse public condemnation and official action.

16. According to the paragraph, all types of illegal conduct are

    A. condemned by all elements of the community
    B. considered a moral offense, although some are tolerated by a few citizens
    C. violations of the law, but some are acceptable to certain elements of the community
    D. found in a social setting which is not punishable by law

17. According to the paragraph, traffic violations are generally considered by society as

    A. crimes requiring the maximum penalty set by the law
    B. more serious than violations of the liquor laws

C. offenses against the morals of the community
D. relatively minor offenses requiring minimum punishment

18. According to the paragraph, a lottery conducted for the purpose of raising funds for a church

    A. is considered a serious violation of law
    B. may be tolerated by a community which has laws against gambling
    C. may be conducted under special laws demanded by the more numerous residents of a community
    D. arouses indignation in most communities

18.____

19. On the basis of the paragraph, the MOST likely reaction in the community to a police raid on a gambling casino would be

    A. more an attitude of indifference than interest in the raid
    B. general approval of the raid
    C. condemnation of the raid by most people
    D. demand for further action since this raid is not sufficient to end gambling activities

19.____

20. The one of the following which BEST describes the central thought of this paragraph and would be MOST suitable as a title for it is

    A. CRIME AND THE POLICE
    B. PUBLIC CONDEMNATION OF GRAFT AND CORRUPTION
    C. GAMBLING IS NOT ALWAYS A VICIOUS BUSINESS
    D. PUBLIC ATTITUDE TOWARD LAW VIOLATIONS

20.____

Questions 21-23.

DIRECTIONS: Answer questions 21 to 23 SOLELY on the basis of the following paragraph.

The law enforcement agency is one of the most important agencies in the field of juvenile delinquency prevention. This is so not because of the social work connected with this problem, however, for this is not a police matter, but because the officers are usually the first to come in contact with the delinquent. The manner of arrest and detention makes a deep impression upon him and affects his life-long attitude toward society and the law. The juvenile court is perhaps the most important agency in this work. Contrary to the general opinion, however, it is not primarily concerned with putting children into correctional schools. The main purpose of the juvenile court is to save the child and to develop his emotional make-up in order that he can grow up to be a decent and well-balanced citizen. The system of probation is the means whereby the court seeks to accomplish these goals.

21. According to this paragraph, police work is an important part of a program to prevent juvenile delinquency because

    A. social work is no longer considered important in juvenile delinquency prevention
    B. police officers are the first to have contact with the delinquent
    C. police officers jail the offender in order to be able to change his attitude toward society and the law
    D. it is the first step in placing the delinquent in jail

21.____

22. According to this paragraph, the CHIEF purpose of the juvenile court is to

    A. punish the child for his offense
    B. select a suitable correctional school for the delinquent
    C. use available means to help the delinquent become a better person
    D. provide psychiatric care for the delinquent

23. According to this paragraph, the juvenile court directs the development of delinquents under its care CHIEFLY by

    A. placing the child under probation
    B. sending the child to a correctional school
    C. keeping the delinquent in prison
    D. returning the child to his home

Questions 24-27.

DIRECTIONS: Answer questions 24 to 27 SOLELY on the basis of the following paragraph.

When a vehicle has been disabled in the tunnel, the officer on patrol in this zone shall press the EMERGENCY TRUCK light button. In the fast lane, red lights will go on throughout the tunnel; in the slow lane, amber lights will go on throughout the tunnel. The yellow zone light will go on at each signal control station throughout the tunnel and will flash the number of the zone in which the stoppage has occurred. A red flashing pilot light will appear only at the signal control station at which the EMERGENCY TRUCK button was pressed. The emergency garage will receive an audible and visual signal indicating the signal control station at which the EMERGENCY TRUCK button was pressed. The garage officer shall acknowledge receipt of the signal by pressing the acknowledgment button. This will cause the pilot light at the operated signal control station in the tunnel to cease flashing and to remain steady. It is an answer to the officer at the operated signal control station that the emergency truck is responding to the call.

24. According to this paragraph, when the EMERGENCY TRUCK light button is pressed,

    A. amber lights will go on in every lane throughout the tunnel
    B. emergency signal lights will go on only in the lane in which the disabled vehicle happens to be
    C. red lights will go on in the fast lane throughout the tunnel
    D. pilot lights at all signal control stations will turn amber

25. According to this paragraph, the number of the zone in which the stoppage has occurred is flashed

    A. immediately after all the lights in the tunnel turn red
    B. by the yellow zone light at each signal control station
    C. by the emergency truck at the point of stoppage
    D. by the emergency garage

26. According to this paragraph, an officer near the disabled vehicle will know that the emergency tow truck is coming when

    A. the pilot light at the operated signal control station appears and flashes red
    B. an audible signal is heard in the tunnel

C. the zone light at the operated signal control station turns red
D. the pilot light at the operated signal control station becomes steady

27. Under the system described in the paragraph, it would be CORRECT to come to the conclusion that

    A. officers at all signal control stations are expected to acknowledge that they have received the stoppage signal
    B. officers at all signal control stations will know where the stoppage has occurred
    C. all traffic in both lanes of that side of the tunnel in which the stoppage has occurred must stop until the emergency truck has arrived
    D. there are two emergency garages, each able to respond to stoppages in traffic going in one particular direction

Questions 28-30.

DIRECTIONS: Answer questions 28 to 30 SOLELY on the basis of the following paragraphs.

In cases of accident, it is most important for an officer to obtain the name, age, residence, occupation, and a full description of the person injured, names and addresses of witnesses. He shall also obtain a statement of the attendant circumstances. He shall carefully note contributory conditions, if any, such as broken pavement, excavation, tights not burning, snow and ice on the roadway, etc. He shall enter all facts in his memorandum book and on Form 17 or Form 18 and promptly transmit the original of the form to his superior officer and the duplicate to headquarters.

An officer shall render reasonable assistance to sick or injured persons. If the circumstances appear to require the services of a physician, he shall summon a physician by telephoning the superior officer on duty and notifying him of the apparent nature of the illness or accident and the location where the physician will be required. He may summon other officers to assist if circumstances warrant.

In case of an accident or where a person is sick on city property, an officer shall obtain the information necessary to fill out card Form 18 and record this in his memorandum book and promptly telephone the facts to his superior officer. He shall deliver the original card at the expiration of his tour to his superior officer and transmit the duplicate to headquarters.

28. According to this quotation, the MOST important consideration in any report on a case of accident or injury is to

    A. obtain all the facts
    B. telephone his superior officer at once
    C. obtain a statement of the attendant circumstances
    D. determine ownership of the property on which the accident occurred

29. According to this quotation, in the case of an accident on city property, the officer should always

    A. summon a physician before filling out any forms or making any entries in his memorandum book
    B. give his superior officer on duty a prompt report by telephone

C. immediately bring the original of Form 18 to his superior officer on duty
D. call at least one other officer to the scene to witness conditions

30. If the procedures stated in this quotation were followed for all accidents in the city, an impartial survey of accidents occurring during any period of time in this city may be MOST easily made by

   A. asking a typical officer to show you his memorandum book
   B. having a superior officer investigate whether contributory conditions mentioned by witnesses actually exist
   C. checking all the records of all superior officers
   D. checking the duplicate card files at headquarters

Questions 31-55.

DIRECTIONS: In each of questions 31 to 55, select the lettered word or phrase which means MOST NEARLY the same as the first word in the row.

31. RENDEZVOUS
    A. parade   B. neighborhood
    C. meeting place D. wander about

32. EMINENT
    A. noted   B. rich   C. rounded   D. nearby

33. CAUSTIC
    A. cheap   B. sweet   C. evil   D. sharp

34. BARTER
    A. annoy   B. trade   C. argue   D. cheat

35. APTITUDE
    A. friendliness   B. talent
    C. conceit   D. generosity

36. PROTRUDE
    A. project B. defend C. choke   D. boast

37. FORTITUDE
    A. disposition   B. restlessness
    C. courage   D. poverty

38. PRELUDE
    A. introduction   B. meaning
    C. prayer   D. secret

39. SECLUSION
    A. primitive   B. influence
    C. imagination   D. privacy

40. RECTIFY
    A. correct   B. construct   C. divide   D. scold

41. TRAVERSE
    A. rotate   B. compose   C. train   D. cross

42. ALLEGE
    A. raise   B. convict   C. declare   D. chase

43. MENIAL
    A. pleasant   B. unselfish
    C. humble   D. stupid

44. DEPLETE
    A. exhaust   B. gather   C. repay   D. close

45. ERADICATE
    A. construct   B. advise   C. destroy   D. exclaim

46. CAPITULATE
    A. cover   B. surrender   C. receive   D. execute

47. RESTRAIN
    A. restore   B. drive   C. review   D. limit

48. AMALGAMATE
    A. join   B. force   C. correct   D. clash

49. DEJECTED
    A. beaten   B. speechless
    C. weak   D. low-spirited

50. DETAIN
    A. hide   B. accuse   C. hold   D. mislead

KEY (CORRECT ANSWERS)

1. A	11. B	21. B	31. C	41. D
2. C	12. D	22. C	32. A	42. C
3. B	13. A	23. A	33. D	43. C
4. C	14. C	24. C	34. B	44. A
5. D	15. D	25. B	35. B	45. C
6. A	16. C	26. D	36. A	46. B
7. B	17. D	27. B	37. C	47. D
8. A	18. B	28. A	38. A	48. A
9. A	19. A	29. B	39. D	49. D
10. C	20. D	30. D	40. A	50. C

TEST 2

DIRECTIONS: Each question or incomplete statement is followed by several suggested answers or completions. Select the one that BEST answers the question or completes the statement. *PRINT THE LETTER OF THE CORRECT ANSWER IN THE SPACE AT THE RIGHT.*

1. AMPLE

   A. necessary   B. plentiful   C. protected   D. tasty

   1.____

2. EXPEDITE

   A. sue   B. omit   C. hasten   D. verify

   2.____

3. FRAGMENT

   A. simple tool   B. broken part
   C. basic outline   D. weakness

   3.____

4. ADVERSARY

   A. thief   B. partner   C. loser   D. foe

   4.____

5. ACHIEVE

   A. accomplish   B. begin   C. develop   D. urge

   5.____

Questions 6-10.

DIRECTIONS: Answer Questions 6 to 10 on the basis of the information given in the table on the following page. The numbers which have been omitted from the table can be calculated from the other numbers which are given.

NUMBER OF DWELLING UNITS CONSTRUCTED

Year	Private one-family houses	In private apt. houses	In public housing	Total dwelling units
1996	4,500	500	600	5,600
1997	9,200	5,300	2,800	17,300
1998	8,900	12,800	6,800	28,500
1999	12,100	15,500	7,100	34,700
2000	?	12,200	14,100	39,200
2001	10,200	26,000	8,600	44,800
2002	10,300	17,900	7,400	35,600
2003	11,800	18,900	7,700	38,400
2004	12,700	22,100	8,400	43,200
2005	13,300	24,300	8,100	45,700
TOTALS	105,900	?	?	?

6. According to this table, the average number of public housing units constructed yearly during the period 1996 through 2005 was

   A. 7,160   B. 6,180   C. 7,610   D. 6,810

   6.____

7. Of the following, the two years in which the number of private one-family homes constructed was GREATEST for the two years together is

   A. 1998 and 1999
   B. 1997 and 2003
   C. 1998 and 2004
   D. 2001 and 2002

8. For the entire period of 1996 through 2005, the total of all private one-family houses constructed exceeded the total of all public housing units constructed by

   A. 34,300   B. 45,700   C. 50,000   D. 83,900

9. Of the total number of private apartment house dwelling units constructed in the ten years given in the table, the percentage which was constructed in 2002 was MOST NEARLY

   A. 5%   B. 11%   C. 16%   D. 21%

10. Considering dwelling units of all types, the average number constructed annually in the period from 2001 through 2005 was GREATER than the average number constructed annually in the period from 1996 through 2000 by

    A. 16,480   B. 33,320   C. 79,300   D. 82,400

11. A car speeds through the toll entrance of a 2 1/4 mile long bridge without paying the toll and reaches the other end of the bridge 1 minute and 30 seconds later. The car was traveling MOST NEARLY at a rate of _____ miles per hour.

    A. 60   B. 70   C. 80   D. 90

12. During one week, 21,500 vehicles passed through the toll booths of a certain bridge. Of these, 550 were buses, 2,230 were trucks, and the rest were passenger cars. The toll charges were $3.50 for a passenger car, $7 for a truck and $14 for a bus. The total income for the week was

    A. $80,850   B. $88,830   C. $102,550   D. $109,550

13. A bullet fired from a revolver travels 100 feet the first second, and each succeeding second it travels a distance 10% less than during the immediately preceding second. The number of feet the bullet will have traveled at the end of the fourth second is MOST NEARLY

    A. 272   B. 320   C. 344   D. 360

14. An officer receives a uniform allowance of $500 a year in a lump sum. Of this amount, he spends $180 for a winter jacket and 40% of the remainder for two pairs of trousers. The officer now wishes to buy a winter overcoat which costs $240.
    The percentage of the purchase price of the overcoat by which he will be short is

    A. 20%   B. 25%   C. 48%   D. 60%

15. It has been suggested that small light cars can be used for certain kinds of police work. These light vehicles can run 30 miles per gallon of gasoline as contrasted with standard cars which run only 15 miles per gallon. Assume gasoline costs the city $3.75 per gallon. During 9,000 miles of travel, use of the small light car in preference to the standard car would result in a saving in gasoline costs of MOST NEARLY

    A. $1,125   B. $1,500   C. $1,875   D. $2,250

3 (#2)

16. Out of a total of 34,750 felony complaints in 2006, 14,200 involved burglary. In 2005, there was a total of 32,300 felony complaints of which 12,800 were burglary.
Of the increase in felonies from 2005 to 2006, the increase in burglaries comprised APPROXIMATELY

 A. 27% B. 37% C. 47% D. 57%

16.____

17. A certain city department has two offices which issue permits, one office handling twice as many applicants as the other. The smaller office grants permits to 40% of its applicants. The larger office handling twice as many applicants grants permits to 60% of its applicants.
If there were 900 applicants at both offices together on a given day, the total number of permits granted by both offices would be MOST NEARLY

 A. 420 B. 450 C. 480 D. 510

17.____

18. If a co-worker is not breathing after receiving an electric shock but is no longer in contact with the electricity, it is MOST important for you to

 A. avoid moving him
 B. wrap the victim in a blanket
 C. start artificial respiration promptly
 D. force him to take hot liquids

18.____

19. Employees using supplies from one of the first-aid kits available throughout the building are required to submit an immediate report of the occurrence.
Logical reasoning shows that the MOST important reason for this report is so that the

 A. supplies used will be sure to be replaced
 B. first-aid kit can be properly sealed again
 C. employee will be credited for his action
 D. record of first-aid supplies will be up-to-date

19.____

20. The BEST IMMEDIATE first-aid treatment for a scraped knee is to

 A. apply plain vaseline   B. wash it with soap and water
 C. apply heat   D. use a knee splint

20.____

21. Artificial respiration after a severe electrical shock is ALWAYS necessary when the shock results in

 A. unconsciousness   B. stoppage of breathing
 C. bleeding   D. a burn

21.____

22. The authority gives some of its maintenance employees instruction in first aid.
The MOST likely reason for doing this is to

 A. eliminate the need for calling a doctor in case of accident
 B. provide temporary emergency treatment in case of accident
 C. lower the cost of accidents to the authority
 D. reduce the number of accidents

22.____

23. The BEST IMMEDIATE first aid if a chemical solution splashes into the eyes is to

 A. protect the eyes from the light by bandaging
 B. rub the eyes dry with a towel

23.____

23

C. cause tears to flow by staring at a bright light
D. flush the eyes with large quantities of clean water

24. If you had to telephone for an ambulance because of an accident, the MOST important information for you to give the person who answered the telephone would be the

    A. exact time of the accident
    B. cause of the accident
    C. place where the ambulance is needed
    D. names and addresses of those injured

25. If a person has a deep puncture wound in his finger caused by a sharp nail, the BEST IMMEDIATE first aid procedure would be to

    A. encourage bleeding by exerting pressure around the injured area
    B. stop all bleeding
    C. prevent air from reaching the wound
    D. probe the wound for steel particles

26. In addition to cases of submersion, artificial respiration is a recommended first aid procedure for

    A. sunstroke   B. electrical shock   C. chemical poisoning   D. apoplexy

27. Assume that you are called on to render first aid to a man injured in an accident. You find he is bleeding profusely, is unconscious, and has a broken arm. There is a strong odor of alcohol about him.
    The FIRST thing for which you should treat him is the

    A. bleeding   B. unconsciousness   C. broken arm   D. alcoholism

28. In applying first aid for removal of a foreign body in the eye, an important precaution to be observed is NOT to

    A. attempt to wash out the foreign body
    B. bring the upper eyelid down over the lower
    C. rub the eye
    D. touch or attempt to remove a speck on the lower lid

29. The one of the following symptoms which is LEAST likely to indicate that a person involved in an accident requires first aid for shock is that

    A. he has fainted twice
    B. his face is red and flushed
    C. his skin is wet with sweat
    D. his pulse is rapid

30. When giving first aid to a person suffering from shock as a result of an auto accident, it is MOST important to

    A. massage him in order to aid blood circulation
    B. have him sip whiskey
    C. prop him up in a sitting position
    D. cover the person and keep him warm

Questions 31-34.

DIRECTIONS: Answer questions 31 to 34 SOLELY on the basis of the following paragraph.

Assume that you are an officer assigned to one large office which issues and receives applications for various permits and licenses. The office consists of one section where the necessary forms are issued; another section where fees are paid to a cashier; and desks where applicants are interviewed and their forms reviewed and completed. There is also a section containing tables and chairs where persons may sit and fill out their applications before being interviewed or paying the fees. your duties consist of answering simple questions, directing the public to the correct section of the office, and maintaining order.

31. A man who speaks English poorly asks you for assistance in obtaining and filling out an application for a permit. You should

    A. send him to an interviewer who can assist him
    B. try to determine what permit he wants and fill out the form for him
    C. refer the man to the office supervisor
    D. ask another applicant to help this person

31.____

32. The office becomes noisy and crowded, with people milling around waiting for service at the various sections.
Of the following, the BEST action for you to take is to

    A. stand in a prominent place and in a loud voice request the people to be quiet
    B. direct all the people not being served to wait at the unoccupied tables until you call them
    C. line up the people in front of each section and keep the lines in good order
    D. tell the people to form a single line outside the office and let in a few at a time

32.____

33. A man who has just been denied a permit becomes angry and shouts that if he "knew the right people" he too could get a permit. His behavior is disturbing the office.
Of the following, the BEST action for you to take is to

    A. order the man to leave at once since his business is done
    B. tell the man to be quiet and file another application
    C. suggest to the supervisor that a pamphlet be prepared explaining the requirements for permits in simple language
    D. ask an interviewer to explain the requirements for his permit to the person and his right of appeal

33.____

34. Just before the close of business, a man rushes in and insists on being interviewed for a permit because his present one expires that night.
Of the following, the BEST action for you to take is to

    A. tell the man that the office is closed
    B. tell the man that there will be no penalty if he returns early the next morning
    C. inquire if an interviewer is still available to take care of him and send him to that desk
    D. tell the cashier to collect the fee and tell the man to return the next morning for an interview

34.____

6 (#2)

35. Fingerprints are often taken of applicants for licenses. Of the following, the MOST valid reason for this procedure is that

   A. the license of someone who commits a crime can be more readily revoked
   B. applicants can be checked for possible criminal records
   C. it helps to make sure that the proper license fee is paid
   D. a complete employment record of the applicant is obtained

35._____

36. Assume that an officer is on patrol at 2 A.M. He notices that the night light inside one of the stores in a public building is out. The store is locked.
Of the following, the FIRST action for him to take at this time is to

   A. continue on his patrol since the light probably burned out
   B. enter the store by any means possible so he can check it
   C. report the matter to his superior
   D. shine his flashlight through the window to look for anything unusual

36._____

37. In questioning a man suspected of having committed a theft, the BEST procedure for an officer to follow is to

   A. induce the man to express his feelings about the police, the courts, and his home environment
   B. threaten him with beatings when he refuses to answer your questions
   C. make any promises necessary to get him to confess
   D. remain calm and objective

37._____

38. As an officer, you are on duty in one of the offices of a large public building. A woman who has just finished her business with this office comes to you and reports that her son who was with her is missing.
The one of the following which is the BEST action for you to take FIRST is to

   A. tell the mother that the child is probably all right and ask her to go to the local police station for help in finding the boy
   B. suggest that the mother wait in the office until the child turns up
   C. check nearby offices in an attempt to locate the child
   D. telephone the local police station and ask if any reports fitting the description of the child have been received

38._____

39. An officer assigned to patrol inside a public building at night has observed two men standing outside the doorway. Of the following, the MOST appropriate action for the officer to take FIRST is to

   A. approach the two men and ask them why they are standing there
   B. hide and wait for the two men to take some action
   C. phone the local police station and ask for help since these men may be planning criminal action
   D. check all the entrance doors of the building to make sure that they are locked

39._____

40. It is standard practice for special officers to inspect the restrooms in public buildings. This is done at regular intervals while on patrol.
Of the following, the BEST reason for this practice is to

   A. inspect sanitary conditions
   B. discourage loiterers and potential criminals

40._____

C. check the ventilation
D. determine if all the equipment and plumbing is working properly

41. While on duty in the evening as an officer assigned to a public building, you receive a report that a card game is going on in one of the offices. Gambling is forbidden on government property.
Of the following, the BEST course of action for you to take is to

A. go to the office and order the card players to leave
B. ignore the complaint since this is probably just harmless social card playing
C. report the matter to the building manager the next day
D. go to the office and, if warranted, issue an appropriate warning

42. It has been suggested that special officers establish good working relationships with the local police officers of the police department on duty in the neighborhood.
Of the following, the MOST valid reason for this practice is that

A. a spirit of good feeling and high morale will be created among members of the police department
B. local police officers will probably cooperate more readily with the special officer
C. local police officers can take over the building patrol duties of the special officer in case he is absent
D. special officers have an even stronger obligation than ordinary citizens to cooperate with the police

43. It has been proposed that an officer assigned to a public building at night remain at one location in the building, instead of walking on patrol through the building.
This proposal is

A. *bad;* chiefly because the officer would probably sit instead of stand at the proper location
B. *good;* chiefly because the officer could do a better job of watching the entire building from one point
C. *bad;* chiefly because anyone seeking to enter the building for illegal purposes might be able to do so at a point other than where the special officer is on duty
D. *good;* chiefly because his supervisors would know exactly where to find him

44. In a busy office, an officer has been assigned the duty of making sure that the public is served in the order of their arrival at the office and that some employee is always taking care of a person desiring help.
Of the following, the BEST method for the officer to follow is to

A. line up the persons in the waiting room
B. give a numbered ticket to each person waiting and call out the numbers, in order, when an employee becomes available
C. loudly announce "next" when an employee is available to serve someone
D. seat one person next to each employee's desk and let the others wait for the first vacant seat

45. Two men have broken into and entered a building at night. The officer on duty at this building sees them, chases them out, and then observes them in the adjoining building. Of the following, the BEST course of action for the officer to take is to

    A. notify the local police station and be ready to aid the police
    B. enter the adjoining building to find the men
    C. notify the manager of his own building
    D. continue on duty since these men have left the building for which he is responsible

46. While an officer is on duty in a crowded waiting room, he finds a woman's purse on the floor.
    Of the following, the FIRST course of action for him to take is to

    A. hold it up in the air, ask who owns it, and give it to whoever claims it
    B. keep the purse until someone claims it
    C. immediately deliver the purse to the "lost and found" desk
    D. ask the lady who is nearest to him if she lost a purse

47. Special officers often have the power of arrest.
    Of the following, the BEST reason for this practice is to

    A. have the officer always arrest any person who refuses to obey his orders
    B. aid in maintaining order in places where he is assigned
    C. promote good public relations
    D. aid in preventing illegal use of public buildings by tenants or employees

48. An officer has told a mother that he found her son writing on the walls of the building with chalk. The mother tells the officer that he should be more concerned with "crooks" than with children's minor pranks.
    Of the following, the BEST answer for the officer to make to this woman is that

    A. children should be taught good conduct by their parents
    B. damage to public property means higher taxes
    C. serious criminals often begin their careers with minor violations
    D. it is his duty to enforce all rules and regulations

49. A man asks you, a special officer, where to get a certain kind of license not issued in your office. You don't know where such licenses are issued.
    Of the following, the BEST procedure for you to follow is to

    A. refer him to the manager of the office
    B. get the information if you can and give it to the man
    C. tell the man to inquire at any police station house
    D. tell the man that you just do not know

50. Special officers are not permitted to ask private citizens to buy tickets for dances or other such social functions, not even when such functions are operated by charitable organizations. Of the following, the BEST reason for this rule is that

    A. private citizens are under no obligation to buy any such tickets
    B. not all groups are allowed equal opportunity in the sale of their tickets
    C. private citizens might complain to officials
    D. private citizens might feel they would not get proper service unless they bought such tickets

KEY (CORRECT ANSWERS)

1. B	11. D	21. B	31. A	41. D
2. C	12. B	22. B	32. C	42. B
3. B	13. C	23. D	33. D	43. C
4. D	14. A	24. C	34. C	44. B
5. A	15. A	25. A	35. B	45. A
6. A	16. D	26. B	36. D	46. C
7. C	17. C	27. A	37. D	47. B
8. A	18. C	28. C	38. C	48. D
9. B	19. A	29. B	39. D	49. B
10. A	20. B	30. D	40. B	50. D

SOLUTIONS TO ARITHMETIC PROBLEMS

11. $2\frac{1}{4}$ miles are completed in 1 1/2 minutes (1 minute and 30 seconds)

    $\therefore 2\frac{1}{4} \div 1\frac{1}{2}$ = rate per minute

    $= \frac{9}{4} \div 1\frac{1}{2}$

    $= \frac{9}{4} \div \frac{3}{2}$

    $= \frac{9}{4} \times \frac{2}{3}$

    $= \frac{3}{2}$ miles per minute

    $\therefore \frac{3}{2} \times 60$ (minutes in an hour) = rate per hour = 90 miles per hour

    (Ans. D)

12. 550 + 2230 = 2780; 21,500 - 2780 = 18,720 passengers

550 buses at $14.00	=	$ 7,700
2230 trucks at $7.00	=	15,610
18720 passengers at $3.50	=	65,520
		$88,830

    (Ans. B)

13. Given: speed = 100 feet the first second

100 - 10 (10% of 100)	=	90 feet - the second second
90 - 9 (10% of 90)	=	81 feet - the third second
81 - 8.1 (10% of 81)	=	72.9 feet - the fourth second
		343.9 (total at end of the fourth second)

    (Ans. C)

14. Given: 500 = uniform allowance

$500 - 180	=	$320	(amount left after buying winter jacket)
$320 x 40%	=	$128	(amount spent for two pairs of trousers)
$320 - 128	=	$192	(amount now left)

    Since the winter overcoat costs $240, he is now short $48 ($240 - 192) or 20% of the purchase price of the overcoat. (48/240 = $\frac{1}{5}$ = 20%)

(Ans. A)

15. Light care: 9000(miles)÷30(miles per gallon)×3.75(per gallon)

$$= \frac{9000}{30} \times 3.75$$
$$= 300 \times 3.75$$
$$= \$1,125 \text{ (total gasoline cost)}$$

Standard cars: 9000 (miles) ÷ 15 (miles per gallon) × 3.75

$$= \frac{9000}{15} \times 3.75$$
$$= 600 \times 3.75$$
$$= \$2,250 \text{ (total gasoline cost)}$$

∴ use of light car would result in a saving in gasoline costs of $1,125 ($2,250 - $1,125).

(Ans. A)

16. 2006:   14,200   (burglary)
    2005:   12,800   (burglary)
            1,400   (increase in burglaries)

    2006:   34,750   (felony)
    2005:   32,300   (felony)
            2,450   (increase in felonies

$$\therefore 1400 \div 2450 = \frac{1400}{2450} = .57$$

WORK

```
          .57
2450 )1400.0
      1225.0
       175.00
       171.50
```

(Ans. D)

17. Given: smaller office: grants permits to 40% of 1/3 of the total number of applicants (900)

    larger office: grants permits to 60% of 2/3 of the total number of applicants (900)

    Solving: smaller office: $.40 \times \frac{1}{3} \times 900 = 120$ permits

    larger office: $.60 \times \frac{2}{3} \times 900 = \underline{360}$ permits
    $\phantom{larger office: .60 \times \frac{2}{3} \times 900 =}$ 480 permits (total)

(Ans. C)

EXAMINATION SECTION
TEST 1

DIRECTIONS: Each question or incomplete statement is followed by several suggested answers or completions. Select the one that BEST answers the question or completes the statement. *PRINT THE LETTER OF THE CORRECT ANSWER IN THE SPACE AT THE RIGHT.*

Questions 1-9.

DIRECTIONS: Questions 1 through 9 are to be answered SOLELY on the basis of the following information and the DIRECTORY OF SERVICES.

Officer Johnson has just been assigned to the North End Service Facility and is now on his post in the main lobby. The facility is open to the public from 9 A.M. to 5 P.M. each Monday through Friday, except on Thursdays when it is open from 9 A.M. to 7 P.M. The facility is closed on holidays.

Officer Johnson must ensure an orderly flow of visitors through the lobby of the facility. To accomplish this, Officer Johnson gives directions and provides routine information to clients and other members of the public who enter and leave the facility through the lobby.

In order to give directions and provide routine information to visitors, such as information concerning the location of services, Officer Johnson consults the Directory of Services shown below. Officer Johnson must ensure that clients are directed to the correct room for service and are sent to that room only during the hours that the particular service is available. When clients ask for the location of more than one service, they should be directed to go first to the service that will close soonest.

NORTH END SERVICE FACILITY
DIRECTORY OF SERVICES

Room	Type of Service	Days Available	Hours Open
101	Facility Receptionist	Monday, Tuesday, Wednesday, Friday	9 AM- 5 PM
		Thursday	9 AM- 7 PM
103	Photo Identification Cards	Monday, Wednesday, Friday	9 AM-12 Noon
104	Lost and Stolen Identification Cards	Wednesday, Thursday	9 AM-5 PM
105	Applications for Welfare/Food Stamps	Wednesday, Friday	1 PM-5 PM
107	Recertification for Welfare/Food Stamps	Monday, Thursday	10 AM- 12 Noon
108	Medicaid Applications	Tuesday, Wednesday	2 PM-5 PM
109	Medicaid Complaints	Tuesday, Wednesday	10 AM-2 PM
110, 111	Social Worker	Monday, Wednesday	9 AM-12 Noon
		Tuesday, Friday	1 PM-5 PM
		Thursday	9 AM- 5 PM
114	Hearing Room (By appointment only)	Monday, Thursday	9 AM-5 PM

DIRECTORY OF SERVICES
(CONT'D)

Room	Type of Service	Days Available	Hours Open
115	Hearing Information	Monday, Tuesday, Wednesday, Thursday, Friday	9 AM-1 PM
206, 207	Nutrition Aid	Monday, Wednesday, Friday Tuesday, Thursday	10 AM-2 PM 9 AM-12 Noon
215	Health Clinic	Monday, Tuesday, Wednesday, Friday Thursday	9 AM-5 PM 9 AM-7 PM
220	Facility Administrative Office	Monday, Tuesday, Wednesday, Thursday, Friday	9 AM-5 PM

1. It is Tuesday morning and Ms. Loretta Rogers, a client of the North End Service Facility, asks Officer Johnson where she should go in order to apply for Medicaid. Officer Johnson tells Ms. Rogers to go to Room _____ at _____.

    A. 108; 1:00 P.M.
    B. 109; 11:00 A.M.
    C. 108; 2:00 P.M.
    D. 109; 2:00 P.M.

2. On Friday at 11:00 A.M., Mrs. Ruth Ramos, a new client at the North End Service Facility, tells Officer Johnson that she wants to obtain a photo identification card and see a social worker.
   Officer Johnson should direct Mrs. Ramos to first go to Room

    A. 103   B. 104   C. 110   D. 220

3. On Friday at 10:30 A.M., a client at the North End Service Facility who is directed by Officer Johnson to go to Room 206 will be able to receive service regarding

    A. Recertification for Welfare/Food Stamps
    B. Hearing Information
    C. Medicaid Applications
    D. Nutrition Aid

4. At 9:00 A.M. on Monday, a client at the North End Service Facility who is directed by Officer Johnson to Room 101 for service will find

    A. Nutrition Aid
    B. Facility Receptionist
    C. Health Clinic
    D. Hearing Information

5. On Tuesday at 12:30 P.M., Mr. Paul Brown tells Officer Johnson that he lost his identification card and wants to obtain a new one as soon as possible.
   Officer Johnson should direct Mr. Brown to go to Room 104

    A. immediately
    B. at 1:00 P.M. that day
    C. at 9:00 A.M. on Wednesday
    D. at 2:00 P.M. on Friday

6. A client at the North End Service Facility explains to Officer Johnson that he wants to make an appointment with a Social Worker.
   The client should be directed to go to Room

   A. 104   B. 110   C. 115   D. 215

7. Ms. Alice Lee is a client at the North End Service Facility who has a 10:00 A.M. appointment on Thursday in the Hearing Room and does not know where to go.
   Officer Johnson should direct Ms. Lee to go to Room

   A. 101   B. 110   C. 112   D. 114

8. Officer Johnson is asked by a visitor which services are available on Thursdays between 5:00 P.M. and 7:00 P.M. Officer Johnson should inform the visitor that an available service during that time is

   A. Health Clinic   B. Medicaid Complaints
   C. Nutrition Aid   D. Social Worker

9. Mr. Jack Klein, a visitor to the North End Service Facility, asks Officer Johnson when and where he can file a complaint concerning Medicaid.
   Officer Johnson should inform Mr. Klein that he may go to Room

   A. 108 on Tuesday or Wednesday between 2:00 P.M. and 5:00 P.M.
   B. 109 on Tuesday or Wednesday between 10:00 A.M. and 2:00 P.M.
   C. 115 on Monday or Tuesday between 10:00 A.M. and 12:00 Noon
   D. 215 on Thursday between 9:00 A.M. and 7:00 P.M.

Questions 10-12.

DIRECTIONS: Questions 10 through 12 are to be answered SOLELY on the basis of the following information.

Security Officers should act in accordance with guidelines included in a manual provided to security staff. Assume that the following guidelines apply to Officers when in contact with visitors or clients in a facility:

1. Try to see things from the visitor's or client's point of view.
2. Ignore insulting comments.
3. Maintain a calm and patient manner.
4. Speak quietly, courteously, and tactfully.

10. Officer Renee Williams is patrolling the lobby area of her facility when she hears a client angrily yelling at the receptionist. She goes to investigate the situation and finds out from the receptionist that the client is one hour late for his appointment with a social worker who now has other appointments. The client demands to be seen by the social worker immediately. Officer Williams angrily tells the client that it is his own fault that he missed his appointment and he should stop bothering the receptionist and go home.
    In this situation, Officer Williams' behavior towards the client is

    A. *proper,* chiefly because it is the client's fault that he missed his appointment
    B. *improper,* chiefly because security officers should stay calm and speak courteously when dealing with clients
    C. *proper,* chiefly because the client had yelled at the receptionist
    D. *improper,* chiefly because the security officer should have ignored the whole incident

11. During his tour, Officer Montgomery is passing through his facility's waiting room on the way to the cafeteria for a break. As Officer Montgomery passes by a visitor, the visitor mutters an insulting remark about the Officer's appearance. Officer Montgomery ignores the visitor and the remark and proceeds on his way to the cafeteria.
Officer Montgomery's action in this situation is

    A. *correct*, chiefly because it is not necessary for Officer Montgomery to respond to visitors while on a break
    B. *incorrect*, chiefly because Officer Montgomery should have ejected the visitor from the facility
    C. *correct*, chiefly because special officers should ignore insults
    D. *incorrect*, chiefly because visitors should not be allowed to ridicule authority figures such as special officers

11.____

12. While patrolling the facility parking lot, Officer Klausner sees an unoccupied car parked in front of a fire hydrant. Officer Klausner writes out a summons for a parking violation and places it on the windshield of the car. As the Officer begins to walk away, the owner of the car spots the summons on the windshield and runs over to the car. The car owner is furious at getting the summons, confronts the Officer, and curses him loudly.
In this situation, Officer Klausner should

    A. curse back at the car owner just as loudly
    B. push him out of the way and resume patrol
    C. calmly explain to him the nature of the violation
    D. return all the insults but in a calm tone

12.____

Question 13.

DIRECTIONS: Question 13 is to be answered SOLELY on the basis of the following information.

Special Officers are permitted to give only general information about social services. They shall not provide advice concerning specific procedures.

13. Special Officer Lynn King is on post near the Medicaid Office in the Manhattan Income Maintenance Center. While Officer King is on post, a client approaches her and asks which forms must be filled out in order to apply for Medicaid benefits. Officer King tells the client that she cannot help him and directs the client to the Medicaid Office.
In this situation, Officer King's response to the client's question is

    A. *correct*, chiefly because Officer King's duties do not include providing any information to clients
    B. *incorrect*, chiefly because Officer King should have provided as much specific information as possible to the client
    C. *correct*, chiefly because Officer King may not advise clients on social services procedures
    D. *incorrect*, chiefly because Officer King should know which forms are used in the facility

13.____

Question 14.

DIRECTIONS: Question 14 is to be answered SOLELY on the basis of the following information.

Security Officers must request that visitors and clients show identification and inspect that identification before allowing them to enter restricted areas in the facility.

14. Security Officer Crane is assigned to a fixed post outside Commissioner Maxwell's office, which is a restricted area. A visitor approaches Officer Crane's desk and states that he is Robert Maxwell and has an appointment with the Commissioner, who is his brother. Officer Crane checks the appointment book, verifies that Robert Maxwell has an appointment with the Commissioner, and allows the visitor to enter the office.
In this situation, Officer Crane's action in allowing the visitor admittance to the Commissioner's office is

    A. *correct*, chiefly because he verified that Robert Maxwell had an appointment with the Commissioner
    B. *incorrect*, chiefly because all visitors must show identification before entering restricted areas
    C. *correct*, chiefly because it would insult the Commissioner's brother if he was asked to show identification
    D. *incorrect*, chiefly because he should have called the Commissioner to verify that he has a brother

14.____

Question 15.

DIRECTIONS: Question 15 is to be answered SOLELY on the basis of the following information.

While on duty, a Special Officer must give his rank, name, and shield number to any person who requests it.

15. Special Officer Karen Mitchell is assigned to patrol an area in the North Bronx Service Facility. While on patrol, Officer Mitchell observes a visitor asking other clients in the lobby for money. Upon investigation, she determines that the visitor has no official business in the facility and asks the visitor to leave the premises. The individual says that he will leave but demands to know Officer Mitchell's name and shield number.
In response to the visitor's demand, Officer Mitchell should

    A. give the individual her name and shield number
    B. inform him that he can only obtain that information from her supervisor
    C. ignore his demand and resume her patrol
    D. tell the visitor that she will issue a summons to him if he keeps bothering her

15.____

Question 16.

DIRECTIONS: Question 16 is to be answered SOLELY on the basis of the following information.

A member of the Security Staff must follow guidelines for providing information to reporters concerning official facility business. Special Officers shall not be interviewed, nor make public speeches or statements pertaining to official business unless authorized. Security Staff must receive authorization from the Office of Public Affairs before speaking to reporters on any matters pertaining to official facility business.

16. You are a Special Officer in a Men's Shelter. A reporter approaches you as you are leaving the building. The reporter requests that you give an insider's view on conditions in the shelter. He assures you that you will remain anonymous.
You should tell the reporter that you

A. must obtain permission from your immediate supervisor before giving any interviews
B. will be more than happy to provide him with information concerning conditions in the shelter
C. must receive authorization from the Office of Public Affairs before giving any interviews
D. may not give him any information, but that your supervisor will be able to provide him with the requested information.

Questions 17-21.

DIRECTIONS: Questions 17 through 21 are to be answered SOLELY on the basis of the following information.

During their tours, Security Officers are required to transmit and receive information and commands over two-way portable radios from other security staff members. Officers use a numbered code to transmit information over the radio. For example, an officer who calls *10-13* into his radio communicates to other officers and supervisors that he is in need of assistance. Assume that the code numbers shown below along with their specified meanings are those used by Special Officers.

Code	Meaning
10-01	Call your command
10-02	Report to your command
10-03	Call Dispatcher
10-04	Acknowledgment
10-05	Repeat message
10-06	Stand-by
10-07	Verify
10-08	Respond to specified area and advise
10-10	Investigate
10-13	Officer needs help
10-20	Robbery in progress
10-21	Burglary in progress
10-22	Larceny in progress
10-24	Assault in progress
10-30	Robbery has occurred

Code	Meaning
10-31	Burglary has occurred
10-34	Assault has occurred
10-40	Unusual incident
10-41	Vehicle accident
10-42	Traffic or parking problem
10-43	Electrical problem
10-50	Dispute or noise
10-52	Disorderly person/group
10-60	Ambulance needed
10-61	Police Department assistance required
10-64	Fire alarm
10-70	Arrived at scene
10-71	Arrest
10-72	Unfounded
10-73	Condition corrected
10-74	Resuming normal duties

17. Officer Cramer is patrolling Parking Lot A when he receives a radio message from Sergeant Wong. Sergeant Wong directs Officer Cramer to respond to Parking Lot B to investigate a reported traffic problem. Upon arriving at Parking Lot B, Officer Cramer observes a vehicle blocking a loading dock so that a delivery truck cannot gain access to the dock. After notification is made to the owner of the vehicle, the vehicle is moved, allowing the delivery truck to gain access to the loading dock. Which of the following should Officer Cramer use to BEST report the events that occurred back to Sergeant Wong?

    A. 10-72, 10-41, 10-73
    B. 10-70, 10-42, 10-73
    C. 10-70, 10-41, 10-74
    D. 10-72, 10-42, 10-74

18. Officer Garret receives a message of *10-24, 10-10* on his radio from his supervisor, Sergeant Gomez. Officer Garret responds to the scene and later sends Sergeant Gomez the following message in response: *10-70, 10-72, 10-74*. Which of the following events are reported by use of those codes?
    Sergeant Gomez ordered Officer Garret to investigate an assault

    A. in progress. Officer Garret arrived at the scene, discovered that the report was unfounded, and resumed normal duties.
    B. that had occurred. Officer Garret arrived at the scene, made an arrest, and then resumed normal duties.
    C. that had occurred. Officer Garret arrived at the scene and discovered that the report was unfounded and resumed normal duties.
    D. in progress. Officer Garret arrived at the scene, made an arrest, and then resumed normal duties.

19. Officer Torres is patrolling the grounds of his facility when he receives a radio message from Sergeant Washington. In response to the radio message, Officer Torres goes to the facility's parking lot and issues a summons to a vehicle blocking an ambulance entrance. The radio message that Officer Torres received from Sergeant Washington is 10-10,

    A. 10-21   B. 10-40   C. 10-42   D. 10-43

20. Officer Oxford transmits the following codes by radio to Sergeant Joseph: *10-20, 10-13*. The response that Officer Oxford receives from Sergeant Joseph on her radio is *10-04*. Which one of the following events are reported by the use of those codes?
    Officer Oxford informed Sergeant Joseph that

    A. a robbery was in progress and that she needs assistance, and Sergeant Joseph acknowledged her message
    B. an assault was in progress and that she wants him to respond to the area, and Sergeant Joseph acknowledged her message
    C. a burglary was in progress and that someone must investigate, and Sergeant Joseph responded that he is standing by
    D. a larceny was in progress and that she needs him to call a dispatcher. Sergeant Joseph reports this incident to his command.

21. While on patrol, Officer Robinson observes that the hall lights in Wing B are flickering on and off. Officer Robinson calls the Maintenance Office and a maintenance worker responds and corrects the problem.
    The radio code that Officer Robinson should transmit to his supervisor to report this incident is

    A. 10-06,10-08   B. 10-40,10-64
    C. 10-43,10-73   D. 10-61,10-07

Question 22.

DIRECTIONS: Question 22 is to be answered SOLELY on the basis of the following information.

The two-way portable radios used by Security or Special Officers to communicate with other security staff members are to be used for official business only. In addition, when transmitting official business, transmission time (time spent transmitting information to other staff) should be kept to a minimum.

22. During his tour, Special Officer Banks calls Sergeant Gates in the patrolroom over the radio and asks if his wife, Alice Banks, had telephoned. Sergeant Gates tells Officer Banks that his wife has not called. Officer Banks then requests that Sergeant Gates notify him as soon as his wife calls because he is expecting an important message concerning his family.
    In this situation, Officer Banks' use of his radio is

    A. *appropriate,* chiefly because his transmission time was not excessive
    B. *inappropriate,* chiefly because he should have made the transmission on his break
    C. *appropriate,* chiefly because his transmission concerned an important family matter
    D. *inappropriate,* chiefly because radios are to be used for official business only

Question 23.

DIRECTIONS: Question 23 is to be answered SOLELY on the basis of the following information.

Special Officers are responsible for monitoring and responding to radio messages, even if the officer is on meal break, performing clerical duties, or away from his post for other reasons. An officer shall answer radio messages directed to him during his tour.

23. Officer Lewis is chatting with friends in the cafeteria while on her scheduled meal break when she receives a radio message from Sergeant Baker. Sergeant Baker informs Officer Lewis that trouble has broken out at Location A and directs her to report to Location A immediately to assist the officers on the scene. Officer Lewis leaves the cafeteria immediately and reports to the scene.
Officer Lewis' action in response to Sergeant Baker's radio message is

 A. *correct,* chiefly because Officer Lewis is responsible for responding to all radio messages
 B. *incorrect,* chiefly because Officer Lewis is on meal break and therefore *off-duty*
 C. *correct,* chiefly because Officer Lewis was not doing anything important during her meal break
 D. *incorrect,* chiefly because the situation was not declared a *total emergency*

Question 24.

DIRECTIONS: Question 24 is to be answered SOLELY on the basis of the following information.

Special Officers must immediately report to their supervisor any incident or condition in the facility that may cause danger or inconvenience to the public.

24. Special Officer Scott is patrolling a small, crowded waiting room in his facility when two male clients start arguing with each other, shoving chairs around and frightening the other clients. Officer Scott intervenes in the argument, issues summonses for Disorderly Conduct to the individuals involved in the dispute, and escorts them off the premises. Officer Scott then records the incident in his memo book and resumes patrol.
In this situation, the FIRST action that Officer Scott should have taken when he observed the argument start between the two men is to

 A. call for help from Special Officers on nearby posts to restrain the men who were fighting
 B. report the incident to his supervisor immediately
 C. attempt to separate the men who were fighting in order to stop the fight
 D. evacuate the waiting room so that innocent bystanders would not be injured

Question 25.

DIRECTIONS: Question 25 is to be answered SOLELY on the basis of the following information.

An Officer on duty in a facility must remain on post until properly relieved. If not properly relieved as scheduled, he must notify his immediate supervisor by radio of this fact and follow the supervisor's instructions.

25. Officer Clough is working on an 8:00 A.M. to 4:00 P.M. tour. Officer Clough is to be relieved at 4:00 P.M. by Security Officer Crandall, who works the 4:00 P.M. to 12:00 Midnight shift. However, as of 4:15 P.M., Officer Crandall has not appeared to relieve Officer Clough, so Officer Clough leaves his post to find Officer Crandall. In this situation, Officer Clough's action is

    A. *correct*, chiefly because his tour was over and he wanted to go home
    B. *incorrect*, chiefly because he should have notified his supervisor of Officer Crandall's failure to relieve him
    C. *correct*, chiefly because Officer Clough is attempting to locate Officer Crandall so that the post will be covered
    D. *incorrect*, chiefly because Officer Clough should have left his post as soon as his tour ended rather than working any overtime

Questions 26-28.

DIRECTIONS: Questions 26 through 28 are to be answered SOLELY on the basis of the following information.

A summons is a written notice that a person is accused of violating a code or regulation. Special Officers have the authority to issue summonses to individuals for on-premises parking or traffic violations, or violations of the City Administrative Code. Summonses for violations of the Penal Law, such as for Disorderly Conduct, may also be issued.

The following is a list of types of summonses issued for violations and their descriptions:

Type of Summons	Description of Violation
Class A	Parking in fire lanes
Class A	Parking in space reserved for the handicapped
Class A	Vehicle blocking driveway
Class B	Disobeying stop sign
Class C	Disorderly Conduct
Class C	Harassment
Environmental Control Board	Smoking Violations
Environmental Control Board	Public Health Code

26. While on patrol, Special Officer Gladys Jones observes a parked car that is blocking a driveway.
She should issue a summons for a violation which is a

    A. Class A type
    B. Class B type
    C. Class C type
    D. Environmental Control Board

27. A man drives up to a facility, parks his car in a fire lane, and quickly runs inside the facility. An attempt to follow and locate the man is unsuccessful.
Which one of the following is the type of summons that the Special Officer on duty should issue?

    A. Class A
    B. Class B
    C. Class C
    D. Environmental Control Board

28. While on patrol, Special Officer Mason observes a visitor smoking a cigarette in an area where smoking is prohibited. Officer Mason asks the visitor to stop smoking and shows him the *No Smoking* sign posted. The visitor refuses to comply.
Officer Mason should issue which type of summons?

    A. Class A
    B. Class B
    C. Class C
    D. Environmental Control Board

Questions 29-31.

DIRECTIONS: Questions 29 through 31 are to be answered SOLELY on the basis of the following information and the Summons Form and Fact Pattern.

Special Officers must complete a summons form by filling in the appropriate information. A completed summons must include the name and address of the accused; license or other identification number; vehicle identification; the section number of the code, regulation, or law violated; a brief description of the violation; any scheduled fine; information about the time and place of occurrence; and the name, rank, and signature of the Special Officer issuing the summons.

The information listed on the Summons Form may or may not be correct.

SUMMONS FORM

LINE	NOTICE OF VIOLATION No. 5 56784989		THE PEOPLE OF THE STATE OF NEW YORK VS.	
1		OPERATOR PRESENT NO (YES) REFUSED ID		
2	LAST NAME *Tucker*	FIRST NAME *James*		MIDDLE INITIAL *T*
3	STREET ADDRESS *205 E. 53rd Street*			
4	CITY (AS SHOWN ON LICENSE) *Brooklyn, NY 11234*			
5	DRIVER LICENSE OR IDENTIFICATION NO. *J-7156907834*	STATE *NY*	CLASS *5*	DATE EXPIRES *1/12/13*
6	SEX *M*	DATE OF BIRTH *1/12/65*		
7	LICENSE PLATE NO. *CVR-632*	STATE *NY*	DATE EXPIRES *8/12/12*	OPERATOR OWN VEHICLE? (YES) NO
8	BODY TYPE *Sedan*	MAKE *Dodge*	COLOR *Green*	
	THE PERSON DESCRIBED ABOVE IS CHARGED AS FOLLOWS:			
9	ISSUE TIME *9:30 A.M.*	DATE OF OFFENSE *2/5/12*	TIME FIRST OBSERVED *9:28 A.M.*	COUNTY *Kings*
10	PLACE OF OCCURRENCE *451 Clarkson Ave., Brooklyn, NY*			PRECINCT *71st*
11	IN VIOLATION OF SECTION *81-B*	CODE *40*	LAW *New York State Traffic Regulation*	
12	DESCRIPTION OF VIOLATION *Vehicle parked in front of a fire hydrant*			
13	SCHEDULED FINE $10 $15 $20 $25 $30 ($40) Other $____			
14	RANK/NAME OF ISSUING OFFICER *Special Officer Joseph Robbins*		SIGNATURE OF ISSUING OFFICER *Joseph Robbins*	

FACT PATTERN

On February 5, 2012, at 9:28 A.M., Special Officer Joseph Robbins is patrolling the grounds of the Brooklyn Hills Income Maintenance Center, located at 451 Clarkson Ave., Brooklyn, NY, when he observes an unoccupied parked vehicle blocking a fire hydrant near the facility's entrance. As Officer Robbins begins to write up a summons for the violation, James Tucker, the owner of the vehicle, emerges from the facility and comes over. While getting in his car, he asks why he is getting a summons. Officer Robbins explains to Mr. Tucker that he is in violation of traffic regulations pertaining to access to fire hydrants and asks him for identification. Mr. Tucker gives Officer Robbins his driver's license, showing the following information:

Name:	Tucker, James T.
Address:	205 E. 53rd Street, Brooklyn, NY 11234
Date of Birth:	January 12, 1965
Driver's License:	J-7156907894
Driver License Expiration Date:	January 12, 2013
Class:	5

29. The *place of occurrence* of the violation described in the Fact Pattern is on line _____ of the Summons Form.

    A. 2   B. 3   C. 8   D. 10

30. Which one of the following lines on the Summons Form shows information that does NOT agree with information given in the Fact Pattern?

    A. 1   B. 2   C. 4   D. 5

31. Which of the following is the date on which the violation occurred?

    A. 1/12/12   B. 2/5/12   C. 8/12/12   D. 1/12/13

32. Following are two sentences which may or may not be written in correct English:
    I. Two clients assaulted the officer.
    II. The van is illegally parked.

    Which one of the following statements is CORRECT?

    A. Only Sentence I is written in correct English.
    B. Only Sentence II is written in correct English.
    C. Sentences I and II are both written in correct English.
    D. Neither Sentence I nor Sentence II is written in correct English.

33. Following are two sentences which may or may not be written in correct English:
    I. Security Officer Rollo escorted the visitor to the patrolroom.
    II. Two entry were made in the facility logbook.

    Which one of the following statements is CORRECT?

    A. Only Sentence I is written in correct English.
    B. Only Sentence II is written in correct English.
    C. Sentences I and II are both written in correct English.
    D. Neither Sentence I nor Sentence II is written in correct English.

34. Following are two sentences which may or may not be written in correct English:
    I. Officer McElroy putted out a small fire in the wastepaper basket.
    II. Special Officer Janssen told the visitor where he could obtained a pass.
Which one of the following statements is CORRECT?

   A. Only Sentence I is written in correct English.
   B. Only Sentence II is written in correct English.
   C. Sentences I and II are both written in correct English.
   D. Neither Sentence I nor Sentence II are written in correct English.

35. Following are two sentences which may or may not be written in correct English:
    I. Security Officer Warren observed a broken window while he was on his post in Hallway C.
    II. The worker reported that two typewriters had been stoled from the office.
Which one of the following statements is CORRECT?

   A. Only Sentence I is written in correct English.
   B. Only Sentence II is written in correct English.
   C. Sentences I and II are both written in correct English.
   D. Neither Sentence I nor Sentence II is written in correct English.

KEY (CORRECT ANSWERS)

1. C
2. A
3. D
4. B
5. C

6. B
7. D
8. A
9. B
10. B

11. C
12. C
13. C
14. B
15. A

16. C
17. B
18. A
19. C
20. A

21. C
22. D
23. A
24. B
25. B

26. A
27. A
28. D
29. D
30. D

31. B
32. C
33. A
34. D
35. A

TEST 2

DIRECTIONS: Each question or incomplete statement is followed by several suggested answers or completions. Select the one that BEST answers the question or completes the statement. *PRINT THE LETTER OF THE CORRECT ANSWER IN THE SPACE AT THE RIGHT.*

Questions 1-5.

DIRECTIONS: Questions 1 through 5 are to be answered SOLELY on the basis of the following information.

Special Officers have the power to arrest members of the public who commit crimes in violation of the Penal Law. Assume that certain classes of crimes covered by various sections of the Penal Law are described below. Special Officers must be able to apply this information when making an arrest in order to accurately determine the type of crime that has been committed.

Crime	Class of Crime	Description of Crime	Section
Petit Larceny	A Misdemeanor	Stealing property worth up to $250	155.25
Grand Larceny 3rd Degree	E Felony	Stealing property worth more than $250	155.30
Grand Larceny 2nd Degree	D Felony	Stealing property worth more than $1,500	155.35
Grand Larceny 1st Degree	C Felony	Stealing property worth any amount of money while making a person fear injury or damage to property	155.40
Assault 3rd Degree	A Misdemeanor	Injuring a person	120.00
Assault 2nd Degree	D Felony	1. Seriously injuring a person; or 2. Injuring an officer of the law	120.05
Assault 1st Degree	C Felony	Seriously injuring a person using a deadly or dangerous weapon	120.10
Disorderly Conduct	Violation	1. Engages in fighting or threatening behavior; or 2. Makes unreasonable noise	240.20
Robbery 3rd Degree	D Felony	Stealing property by force	160.05
Robbery 2nd Degree	C Felony	1. Stealing property by force with the help of another person; or 2. Stealing property by force and injuring any person	160.10
Robbery 1st Degree	B Felony	Stealing property by force and seriously injuring the owner of property	160.15

2 (#2)

1. Which one of the following crimes is considered to be Class A Misdemeanor? 1.____

   A. Grand Larceny - 3rd Degree
   B. Grand Larceny - 2nd Degree
   C. Assault - 3rd Degree
   D. Assault - 2nd Degree

2. Which one of the following crimes is considered to be Class B Felony? 2.____

   A. Robbery - 2nd Degree
   B. Robbery - 1st Degree
   C. Grand Larceny - 3rd Degree
   D. Grand Larceny - 2nd Degree

3. A worker at a facility reports that a typewriter worth $400 has been stolen from her office. Which one of the following is the type of crime that has been committed? 3.____

   A. Grand Larceny - 3rd Degree
   B. Grand Larceny - 2nd Degree
   C. Grand Larceny - 1st Degree
   D. Petit Larceny

4. A visitor at a facility begins yelling very loudly at a receptionist and shakes his fist at her. The visitor refuses to stop yelling when an officer tries to calm him down, and he shakes his fist at the officer. Which one of the following is the type of crime that occurred? 4.____

   A. Assault - 3rd Degree   B. Assault - 2nd Degree
   C. Assault - 1st Degree   D. Disorderly Conduct

5. An officer has apprehended and arrested a visitor who was attempting to leave the facility with a radio he had stolen from an office. The radio is worth $100.
   Under which one of the following sections of the Penal Law should the visitor be charged? Section 5.____

   A. 155.25   B. 155.30   C. 155.35   D. 155.40

Questions 6-12.

DIRECTIONS: Questions 6 through 12 are to be answered SOLELY on the basis of the Arrest Report Form and Incident Report shown on the following page. These reports were submitted by Special Officer John Clark, Shield #512, to his supervisor, Sergeant Joseph Lewis, Shield #818, of the North Bay Health Clinic

Special Officers are required to complete both an Arrest Report Form and an Incident Report whenever an unusual incident or an arrest occurs. The Arrest Report Form provides detailed information regarding the victim and the person arrested, along with a brief description of the incident.

The Incident Report provides a detailed description of the incident. Both reports include the following information: WHO was involved in the incident, including witnesses; WHAT happened and HOW it happened; WHERE and WHEN the incident occurred; and WHY the incident occurred.

ARREST REPORT FORM

ARREST INFORMATION (1)	TIME OF OCCURRENCE 11:15 A.M.	DATE OF OCCURRENCE February 1, 2012	DAY OF WEEK Monday	
INFORMATION ABOUT VICTIM (2)	VICTIM'S NAME Darlene Kirk	ADDRESS 7855 Cruger St., Bronx, NY 10488		
(3)	SEX F	DATE OF BIRTH 9/3/75	RACE White	HOME TELEPHONE # 212-733-3462	SOCIAL SECURITY # 245-63-0772
INFORMATION ABOUT PERSON ARRESTED (4)	NAME OF PERSON ARRESTED Elsie Gardner	ADDRESS 2447 Southern Pkway, Bronx, NY 10467		
(5)	SEX F	DATE OF BIRTH 7/9/80	RACE White	HOME TELEPHONE # 212-513-7029	SOCIAL SECURITY # 244-08-0569
(6)	HEIGHT 5'5"	WEIGHT 135 lbs.	HAIR COLOR Brown	CLOTHING Black coat/red pants	
DESCRIPTION OF CRIME (7)	SECTION OF PENAL LAW 120.00	TYPE OF CRIME Assault - 3rd Degree		
(8)	TIME OF ARREST 11:35 A.M.	DATE OF ARREST 2/1/12	LOCATION OF ARREST 635 Bay Avenue Bronx, NY	
(9)	DESCRIPTION OF INCIDENT The defendant, Elsie Gardner, struck the victim after the victim requested that Ms. Gardner stop smoking in a "NO SMOKING" area. Two witnesses verified the victim's account of the incident.			
INFORMATION ABOUT ARRESTING OFFICER (10)	REPORTING OFFICER'S SIGNATURE *John Clark*	NAME PRINTED John Clark		
(11)	RANK Special Officer	SHIELD NUMBER 512		

INCIDENT REPORT

(1) At 11:15 A.M. on February 1, 2012, I was directed by Sergeant Mark Lewis via two-way radio to report to the Nutrition Clinic on the 4th Floor to investigate a disturbance. (2) Special Officer Anna Colon, Shield #433, was directed to assist me. (3) At 11:16 A.M., Officer Colon and I arrived at the Health Clinic and observed a patient, Elsie Gardner, repeatedly strike Health Clinic receptionist Darlene Kirk about the head and neck. (4) Officer Colon restrained Ms. Gardner while I placed handcuffs on her wrists. (5) Ms. Kirk complained that her neck felt sore. (6) After being examined by Dr. Stone, Ms. Kirk told us that Ms. Gardner entered the Health Clinic at approximately 11:10 A.M. and lit a cigarette in the waiting area. (7) At 11:20 A.M., Dr. Paul Stone examined Ms. Kirk. (8) Ms. Kirk explained to Ms. Gardner that smoking was not allowed in the Health Clinic and showed her the *NO SMOKING* signs posted on the walls. (9) Ms. Gardner ignored Ms. Kirk, and then grew very abusive and attacked her when Ms. Kirk insisted that she stop smoking. (10) Two witnesses, patients Edna Manning of 8937 4th Ave., Bronx, NY, and John Schultz of 357 149th Street, Bronx, NY, gave the same account of the incident as Ms. Kirk. (11) At 11:30 A.M., I read the prisoner her rights and placed her under arrest for violation of Penal Law Section 120.00 -Assault 3rd Degree. (12) At 11:35 A.M., I notified the 86th Precinct of Ms. Gardner's arrest and arranged for the transportation of the prisoner to the precinct. (13) At 11:40 A.M., Officer Colon escorted Ms. Gardner from the Nutrition Clinic to the patrolroom. (14) At 11:55 A.M., Police Officers Cranford, Shield #658, and Wargo, Shield #313, arrived at the facility to transport the prisoner to the precinct. (15) Officer Gray, Shield #936, assumed my post while I reported to the patrolroom to complete the necessary forms concerning the arrest.

6. At what time did Sergeant Lewis inform Officer John Clark of the disturbance in the Nutrition Clinic?
   _____ A.M.

   A. 11:00   B. 11:15   C. 11:16   D. 11:20

7. According to the Arrest Report and the Incident Report, how many witnesses gave the same account of the incident as Ms. Kirk?

   A. 1   B. 2   C. 3   D. 4

8. What information on the Arrest Report is NOT included in the Incident Report?

   A. Date of Occurrence
   B. Victim's address
   C. Section of the Penal Law violated
   D. Assault 3rd Degree

9. Which sentence in the Incident Report is out of order in terms of the sequence of events?

   A. 3   B. 6   C. 11   D. 12

10. According to the Incident Report, at 11:40 A.M. Ms. Gardner was

    A. escorted to the patrolroom
    B. transported to the 86th Precinct
    C. examined by Dr. Paul Stone
    D. giving an account of the incident to Special Officers Clark and Colon

11. According to the Incident Report, which one of the following officers relieved Officer Clark?
    Officer

    A. Colon   B. Cranford   C. Wargo   D. Gray

12. Which section of the Arrest Report contains information that does NOT agree with Sentence 11 of the Incident Report?
    Section

    A. 1   B. 7   C. 8   D. 9

Question 13.

DIRECTIONS: Question 13 is to be answered SOLELY on the basis of the following information.

A Security Officer must investigate any complaint or incident which occurs in the facility, whether he considers it is major or minor. The Officer must also interview the person(s) involved in the incident in order to complete the necessary forms and reports.

13. Ms. Peters, a clerical worker at the facility, complains to Officer Tynan that a pen set, which had been given to her as a gift, was missing from her desk. She tells Officer Tynan that she knows the pen set was on her desk the previous day because she was using it for her work. Officer Tynan informs Ms. Peters that there is nothing he can do since the pen set was personal property and not facility property.
In this situation, Officer Tynan's response to Ms. Peters is

   A. *correct,* chiefly because the pen set should not have been left out on a desk where it could be stolen
   B. *incorrect,* chiefly because a complaint of a loss of theft should be investigated and recorded
   C. *correct,* chiefly because Special Officers are only required to investigate a loss or theft of facility property
   D. *incorrect,* chiefly because Ms. Peters' work required use of the pen set

Question 14.

DIRECTIONS: Question 14 is to be answered SOLELY on the basis of the following information.

Assume that Security Officers are responsible for recording in a personal memobook all of their routine and non-routine activities and occurrences for each tour of duty. Before starting a tour of duty, a Security Officer must enter in his personal memobook the date, tour, and assigned post. An entry shall be made to record each absence from duty, such as a regular day off, sick leave, annual leave, or holiday. During each tour, a Security Officer shall enter a full and accurate record of duties performed, changes in post assignment, absences from post, and the reason for each absence, and all other patrol business.

14. Security Officer Ella Lewis is assigned to Gotham Center Facility, where she works Monday through Friday on a 9:00 A.M. to 5:00 P.M. tour. Officer Lewis' regular days off are Saturday and Sunday. Officer Lewis worked on Wednesday, November 25, 2012. She was absent on Thursday, November 26, 2012, for Thanksgiving Holiday, and on Friday, November 27, 2012, for annual leave.
According to the information given above, which of the following entries is the FIRST entry that Officer Lewis should record in her memobook when she returns to work on November 30, 2012?

   A. Saturday, 11/28/12 and Sunday, 11/29/12 - Regular days off
   B. Friday, 11/27/12 - Sick Leave
   C. Monday, 11/30/12 - On duty
   D. Thursday, 11/26/12 - Thanksgiving Holiday

Questions 15-16.

DIRECTIONS: Questions 15 and 16 are to be answered SOLELY on the basis of the following entries recorded by Security Officer Angela Russo in her memobook.

Date: January 8, 2012
Tour: 8:00 A.M. to 4:00 P.M.
Weather: Sunny and clear

7:30	Reported to *B* Command for Roll Call. Assigned to Post #2, *C* Building Emergency Room Corridor by Sergeant Robert Floyd. Break: 9:30 A.M. Meal: 1:30 P.M. Radio: #701
7:40	Arrived at Post #2 and relieved Special Officer Johnson, Shield #593.
7:45	On patrol - Post #2.
8:00	Post #2 - All secure at this time; conditions normal.
8:30	Fire Alarm Box 5-3-1 rings on 3rd Floor South in *C* Building. Upon arrival, Office Worker Molly Lewis reported that a waste-paper basket was on fire. Used fire extinguisher to put out fire.
8:50	Condition corrected; Incident Report prepared and submitted to Sergeant Floyd in *B* Command.
8:55	Resumed patrol of Post #2.
9:30	Relieved for break by Officer Tucker.
9:50	Resumed patrol of Post #2.
10:10	Disorderly person reported by Clinic Director Lila Jones on Ward C-32; Officer Bailey and myself responded. Clinic Director Jones informed officers that visitor Bradley Manna, male white, 19 years of age, 2 Park Place, Brooklyn, NY, is drunk and has been shouting insults to Clinic staff.
10:30	Condition corrected; Visitor Bradley Manna escorted off premises. *B* Command notified of incident.
10:40	Resumed patrol of Post #2.
11:40	Post #2 - All secure at this time.
12:40	Post #2 - All secure at this time.

15. The name of the Clinic Director who reported a disorderly person is

    A. Molly Lewis   B. Bradley Manna
    C. Lila Jones   D. Robert Floyd

15.____

16. Which of the following sets of officers responded to the report of a disorderly person on Ward C-32?
Officers

    A. Johnson and Bailey   B. Russo and Tucker
    C. Johnson and Tucker   D. Russo and Bailey

16.____

17. Security Officer Mace is completing an entry in her memo-book. The entry has the following five sentences:
    1. I observed the defendant removing a radio from a facility vehicle.
    2. I placed the defendant under arrest and escorted him to the patrolroom.
    3. I was patrolling the facility parking lot.
    4. I asked the defendant to show identification.
    5. I determined that the defendant was not authorized to remove the radio.
    The MOST logical order for these sentences to be entered in Officer Mace's memo-book is

    A. 1, 3, 2, 4, 5
    B. 2, 5, 4, 1, 3
    C. 3, 1, 4, 5, 2
    D. 4, 5, 2, 1, 3

18. Security Officer Riley is completing an entry in his memo-book. The entry has the following five sentences:
    1. Anna Jones admitted that she stole Mary Green's wallet.
    2. I approached the women and asked them who they were and why they were arguing.
    3. I arrested Anna Jones for stealing Mary Green's wallet.
    4. They identified themselves and Mary Green accused Anna Jones of stealing her wallet.
    5. I was in the lobby area when I observed two women arguing about a wallet.
    The MOST logical order for these sentences to be entered
    in Officer Riley's memobook is

    A. 2, 4, 1, 3, 5
    B. 3, 1, 4, 5, 2
    C. 4, 1, 5, 2, 3
    D. 5, 2, 4, 1, 3

19. Assume that Security Officer John Ryan is completing an entry in his memobook. The entry has the following five sentences:
    1. I then cleared the immediate area of visitors and staff.
    2. I noticed smoke coming from a broom closet outside Room A71.
    3. Sergeant Mueller arrived with other officers to assist in clearing the area.
    4. Upon investigation, I determined the smoke was due to burning material in the broom closet.
    5. I pulled the corridor fire alarm and notified Sergeant Mueller of the fire.
    The MOST logical order for these sentences to be entered in Officer Ryan's memo-book is

    A. 2, 3, 4, 5, 1
    B. 2, 4, 5, 1, 3
    C. 4, 1, 2, 3, 5
    D. 5, 3, 2, 1, 4

20. Security Officer Hernandez is completing an entry in his memobook. The entry has the following five sentences:
    1. I asked him to leave the premises immediately.
    2. A visitor complained that there was a strange man loitering in Clinic B hallway.
    3. I went to investigate and saw a man dressed in rags sitting on the floor of the hallway.
    4. As he walked out, he started yelling that he had no place to go.
    5. I asked to see identification, but he said that he did not have any.
    The MOST logical order for these sentences to be entered in Officer Hernandez's memobook is

| A. 2, 3, 5, 1, 4 | B. 3, 1, 2, 4, 5 |
| C. 4, 1, 5, 2, 3 | D. 3, 1, 5, 2, 4 |

21. Officer Hogan is completing an entry in his memobook. The entry has the following five sentences:
    1. When the fighting had stopped, I transmitted a message requesting medical assistance for Mr. Perkins.
    2. Special Officer Manning assisted me in stopping the fight.
    3. When I arrived at the scene, I saw a client, Adam Finley strike a facility employee, Peter Perkins.
    4. As I attempted to break up the fight, Special Officer Manning came on the scene.
    5. I received a radio message from Sergeant Valez to investigate a possible fight in progress in the waiting room.

    The MOST logical order for these sentences to be entered in Officer Hogan's memobook is

    | A. 2, 1, 4, 5, 3 | B. 3, 5, 2, 4, 1 |
    | C. 4, 5, 3, 1, 2 | D. 5, 3, 4, 2, 1 |

Questions 22-23.

DIRECTIONS: Questions 22 and 23 are to be answered SOLELY on the basis of the following information.

Assume that Security Officers may be assigned to the facility patrolroom and must follow the guidelines below in documenting all routine and non-routine activities and occurrences in the facility logbook.

At the beginning of each tour of duty, the Security Officer responsible for entering information in the logbook must transfer from the Roll Call Sheet to the logbook a list of all security staff personnel assigned to that tour. This list is to be entered in order of the rank of the security staff member. All other entries in the facility logbook shall be recorded in chronological order, in blue or black ink, and be neat and legible.

22. When recording the list of security staff personnel assigned to a tour, that entry shall be made in

    A. chronological order
    B. order of rank of security staff
    C. alphabetical order
    D. order of arrival at facility

23. A Security Officer has transmitted notification to the patrolroom that he has just issued a summons. The Security Officer responsible for documenting occurrences in the patrolroom logbook should record the information

    A. in red ink, immediately following the previous entry
    B. on a new page under the heading *Summonses Reported*
    C. in blue or black ink immediately following the previous entry
    D. on the last page of the logbook where it can be easily found

Question 24.

DIRECTIONS: Question 24 is to be answered SOLELY on the basis of the following information.

Assume that whenever a Security Officer is to begin a leave of absence, long-term sick leave, or other type of leave having an anticipated length of ten days or more, the officer shall surrender his or her security shield to his supervisor, who shall immediately forward it to Security Headquarters.

24. Two male clients were fighting in the waiting room of North End Hospital. Officer Gary Klott attempted to separate them and became involved in the altercation. Officer Klott sustained an injury to the right eye and was examined by a physician. The physician directed Officer Klott to stay home for a recovery period of 12 days. In this situation, Officer Klott should

   A. surrender his shield to his supervisor
   B. safeguard his shield in a safe place at home while he is recovering
   C. surrender his shield to the physician
   D. safeguard his shield with his uniform in his locker at the facility while he is recovering

Question 25.

DIRECTIONS: Question 25 is to be answered SOLELY on the basis of the following information.

Assume that Security Officers are required to follow certain procedures when on post at a restricted area of a facility. They must inspect the identification of employees and passes of visitors, as well as all bags and packages carried by individuals who wish to enter the restricted area.

25. Security Officer Stevens is assigned to a post at the Intensive Care Unit of Park View Hospital, a restricted area. Officer Stevens is responsible for inspecting identification and passes, as well as all bags and packages carried by individuals who want to enter the Unit. He sees Mr. Craig approach. He knows Mr. Craig's wife is a patient in the Unit. Officer Stevens has seen Mr. Craig visit his wife every day for the past four days. Mr. Craig brings a small duffel bag filled with magazines each time he comes. Today, Officer Stevens checks Mr. Craig's visitor's pass but lets Mr. Craig enter the Unit without checking his duffel bag. In this situation, Officer Stevens' action is

   A. *correct*, chiefly because he has checked to see that Mr. Craig has a visitor's pass
   B. *incorrect*, chiefly because all packages and bags must be inspected before anyone is allowed to enter a restricted area
   C. *correct*, chiefly because he is familiar with Mr. Craig and knows that he only carries magazines in his duffel bag
   D. *incorrect*, chiefly because Mr. Craig should not be allowed to carry a bag or package into a restricted area of the facility

Question 26.

DIRECTIONS: Question 26 is to be answered SOLELY on the basis of the following information.

Assume that Special Officers must safeguard evidence in cases involving firearms. Special Officers must mark recovered bullets for identification purposes. The Officer who recovers the bullet must mark his or her initials and the date of recovery of the bullet on the base or on the nose of the bullet.

26. On January 18, 2012, at 11:30 P.M., an unidentified person fired a shot at an unoccupied security patrol car in the facility parking lot. Officer Debra Johnson was assigned to investigate the matter. A fired bullet was recovered inside the patrol car by Officer Johnson at 1:00 A.M. on January 19, 2012.
Officer Johnson should mark *D.J. 1/19/12* on

    A. the base or the nose of the recovered bullet
    B. the side of the recovered bullet
    C. an envelope and place the recovered bullet inside
    D. the side of the patrol car from which the bullet was recovered

26.___

Question 27.

DIRECTIONS: Question 27 is to be answered SOLELY on the basis of the following information.

Patrolroom Observers are officers who are assigned to observe events when individuals, other than security staff, are present in the patrolroom. According to facility guidelines, a Patrolroom Observer must be called to the patrolroom to serve as a witness whenever any individual is brought to the patrolroom for any reason by a Special Officer.

27. Janet Childs, a client at Gotham Health Facility, was robbed in the facility's parking lot. Ms. Childs was not harmed as a result of the incident, but she was upset. Special Officer Grey escorted her to the patrol-room, where she remained until she felt better. While she was waiting in the patrolroom, Officer Grey did not call a Patrolman Observer to the patrolroom during the time that Ms. Childs was there.
In this situation, Officer Grey

    A. should not have taken Ms. Childs to the patrolroom without special authorization from his supervisor
    B. was not required to call a Patrolroom Observer to the patrolroom since Ms. Childs had not been placed under arrest
    C. should have called a Patrolroom Observer to be present while Ms. Childs was in the patrolroom
    D. should have escorted Ms. Childs to the patrolroom and left her in the care of the Special Officer assigned to the patrolroom

27.___

Question 28.

DIRECTIONS: Question 28 is to be answered SOLELY on the basis of the following information.

Special Officers escort individuals categorized as Emotionally Disturbed Persons to the hospital for observation or treatment when directed to do so. These individuals are transported to the hospital by Emergency Medical Service (EMS) ambulance. There must be one Special Officer present in the ambulance for each Emotionally Disturbed Person transferred to the hospital, along with an EMS Technician and the ambulance driver.

28. Special Officers Patrick Lawson and Grace Martin have been assigned to escort two individuals categorized as Emotionally Disturbed Persons from that facility to a nearby hospital. The EMS ambulance, with an EMS Technician and ambulance driver, has arrived at the facility to transport the individuals. Officer Lawson then suggests to Officer Martin that it is not necessary for him to go to the hospital since the EMS Technician will be with Officer Martin in the ambulance.
In this situation, Officer Lawson's suggestion is

    A. *correct*, since an EMS Technician will be present in the ambulance to accompany Officer Martin and the Emotionally Disturbed Persons to the hospital
    B. *incorrect*, since one Special Officer must be present in the ambulance for each Emotionally Disturbed Person transported to the hospital
    C. *correct*, since the Emotionally Disturbed Persons are unlikely to cause any disturbance inside the ambulance
    D. *incorrect*, since two EMS Technicians must be present in the ambulance when only one Special Officer is escorting two Emotionally Disturbed Persons to the hospital

28.____

Questions 29-32.

DIRECTIONS: Questions 29 through 32 are to be answered on the basis of the following information.

Assume that information concerning new or updated policies and procedures are sometimes provided to facility security staff in the form of a memorandum from Security Headquarters.

Question 29.

DIRECTIONS: Question 29 is to be answered SOLELY on the basis of the following memorandum.

TO: All Security Officers
FROM: Security Headquarters
SUBJECT: Smoking Regulations

At times, Security Officers have been observed smoking while on duty at their assigned posts. This is strictly prohibited. If Officers feel that they must smoke, they may smoke during breaks or lunch period in designated areas. Officers may not smoke while on official duty. If any Officer is observed smoking while on post or while performing official duties, appropriate disciplinary action will be taken.

29. According to the above memorandum, Security Officers may

    A. smoke while on duty, as long as they are out of view of the public
    B. not smoke while on duty except when assigned to a post in a designated smoking area
    C. smoke on breaks or during lunch period in designated areas
    D. not smoke at any time when dressed in official uniform

Question 30.

DIRECTIONS: Question 30 is to be answered SOLELY on the basis of the following memorandum.

TO: All Special Officers
FROM: Security Headquarters
SUBJECT: Safeguarding Shields and Identification Cards

Special Officers must ensure that their shields and identification cards are secure at all times. Should an officer become aware of the loss or theft of his shield or identification card, he shall immediately report such loss or theft to Security Headquarters.

30. According to the above memorandum, a Special Officer must

    A. report the loss or theft of his identification card to the nearest police precinct
    B. secure his shield in his locker at all times
    C. report the loss or theft of his shield or identification card to Security Headquarters immediately
    D. secure his identification card at Security Headquarters each night before leaving the facility

Question 31.

DIRECTIONS: Question 31 is to be answered SOLELY on the basis of the following memorandum.

TO: All Security Officers
FROM: Security Headquarters
SUBJECT: Fire in the Facility

Special Officers must report immediately to assist at the scene of a fire when directed to do so by a supervisor. Officers shall remain at the scene and ensure that only authorized personnel are in an area restricted by a fire emergency. Visitors and clients shall be directed to the nearest safe stairwell and out of the facility. Visitors and clients are not to use elevators to evacuate the area.

31. According to the above memorandum, a Security Officer should

    A. direct visitors and clients to the nearest elevator in case of fire
    B. report unauthorized personnel at a fire scene to the Fire Department
    C. escort visitors and clients down the nearest stairwell and out of the facility
    D. ensure that only authorized personnel are in an area restricted by a fire emergency

Question 32.

DIRECTIONS: Question 32 is to be answered SOLELY on the basis of the following memorandum.

TO: All Security Officers
FROM: Security Headquarters
SUBJECT: Reporting Unsafe Conditions

Security Officers shall report to their supervisors and appropriate facility staff any condition that could affect the safety or security of the facility. Conditions such as broken windows, unlocked doors and water leaks should be reported.

32. According to the above memorandum, a Security Officer shall

   A. make recommendations to his superiors concerning other facility staff members
   B. correct all unsafe conditions such as broken windows
   C. report a condition such as a water leak to his supervisor and appropriate facility staff
   D. make recommendations to facility staff concerning doors to be left unlocked

33. Following are two sentences that may or may not be written in correct English:
   I. Special Officer Cleveland was attempting to calm an emotionally disturbed visitor.
   II. The visitor did not stops crying and calling for his wife.
   Which one of the following statements is CORRECT?

   A. Only Sentence I is written in correct English.
   B. Only Sentence II is written in correct English.
   C. Sentences I and II are both written in correct English.
   D. Neither Sentence I nor Sentence II is written in correct English.

34. Following are two sentences that may or may not be written in correct English:
   I. While on patrol, I observes a vagrant loitering near the drug dispensary.
   II. I escorted the vagrant out of the building and off the premises.
   Which one of the following statements is CORRECT?

   A. Only Sentence I is written in correct English.
   B. Only Sentence II is written in correct English.
   C. Sentences I and II are both written in correct English.
   D. Neither Sentence I nor Sentence II is written in correct English.

35. Following are two sentences that may or may not be written in correct English:
   I. At 4:00 P.M., Sergeant Raymond told me to evacuate the waiting area immediately due to a bomb threat.
   II. Some of the clients did not want to leave the building.
   Which one of the following statements is CORRECT?

   A. Only Sentence I is written in correct English.
   B. Only Sentence II is written in correct English.
   C. Sentences I and II are both written in correct English.
   D. Neither Sentence I nor Sentence II is written in correct English.

KEY (CORRECT ANSWERS)

1.	C	16.	D
2.	B	17.	C
3.	A	18.	D
4.	D	19.	B
5.	A	20.	A
6.	B	21.	D
7.	B	22.	B
8.	B	23.	C
9.	B	24.	A
10.	A	25.	B
11.	D	26.	A
12.	C	27.	C
13.	B	28.	B
14.	D	29.	C
15.	C	30.	C

31.	D
32.	C
33.	A
34.	B
35.	C

EXAMINATION SECTION
TEST 1

DIRECTIONS: Each question or incomplete statement is followed by several suggested answers or completions. Select the one that *BEST* answers the question or completes the statement. *PRINT THE LETTER OF THE CORRECT ANSWER IN THE SPACE AT THE RIGHT.*

1. When a security officer fails to report to work in time to make his scheduled relief, the security officer on duty must call the foreman immediately.
   The *MAIN* reason for this procedure is to

   A. make sure that the security officer on duty is not overworked
   B. make a record of the number of times that a security officer is late
   C. make sure that Authority property and materials are continuously guarded
   D. prevent the security officer who is late from being paid for the time that he did not work

2. A security officer must report to his foreman any employee who is on Authority property in an intoxicated condition.
   The *MAIN* reason for this procedure is that

   A. this employee may give the general public the impression that many Authority employees drink while on duty
   B. an employee who drinks on the job may encourage fellow employees to also drink on the job
   C. an intoxicated employee may endanger himself and other Authority employees
   D. the intoxicated employee's foreman may not have noticed this condition

3. If a security officer is required to make hourly calls to his foreman within twenty minutes of the hour, a correct time for a security officer to make his hourly call is at

   A. 3:36 A.M.   B. 8:29 A.M.   C. 4:27 A.M.   D. 7:48 P.M.

4. Which of the following characteristics of a security officer doing record keeping is *MOST* important?

   A. Familiarity with rules and procedures
   B. An analytical mind
   C. Accuracy
   D. Speed

5. Of the following, the type of equipment that a security officer working a 12:00 midnight to 8:00 A.M. shift would be expected to use *MOST* often is a

   A. pistol   B. flashlight   C. camera   D. siren

6. Before going on duty, a security officer is required to read all new bulletins posted on the bulletin board. The *MAIN* reason for this requirement is to

   A. acquaint the security officer with new regulations
   B. make sure that the security officer understands all the rules
   C. make the security officer responsible for any violations of the rules
   D. acquaint the security officer with his rights

7. Assume that soon after being appointed as a security officer, you decide that some of the rules and regulations of the Authority are unwise.
Of the following, you should

   A. disregard these rules and regulations and use your own good judgment
   B. not do your job until some changes are made
   C. make the changes that you decide are necessary
   D. carry out these rules and regulations regardless of your opinion

Questions 8-11.
DIRECTIONS: Questions 8 to 11 are based on information contained in LOCATION OF KEY STATIONS shown below. When answering these questions, refer to this information.

LOCATION OF KEY STATIONS

No. 12 key station - located on double fire exit door adjacent to Briarcliff Avenue vehicle ramp.
No. 13 key station - located on wall adjacent to fire exit door in Unit Repair Section.
No. 14 key station - located in men's locker room on door leading to washroom near water cooler.
No. 15 key station - located in corridor leading to transportation area on wall adjacent to room number 1 and opposite to first aid room.
No. 16 key station - located on wall adjacent to door leading into unit storeroom.
No. 17 key station - located on a wall adjacent to double fire exit doors in Unit Repair Section.
No. 18 key station - located on wall adjacent to fire exit door in body shop.

8. Two key stations are located on or near double fire exit doors. One of them is key station No. 12.
The *other* is key station No.

   A. 13   B. 14   C. 17   D. 18

9. If a security officer took a drink of water, he would MOST likely do so at a location closest to key station No.

   A. 12   B. 14   C. 16   D. 17

10. A delivery of $759.00 worth of supplies would MOST likely be made to a location which is closest to key station No.

   A. 13   B. 14   C. 16   D. 18

11. A fire exit door will NOT be found at key station No.

   A. 12   B. 13   C. 15   D. 17

12. When preparing a report, a security officer should generally make *at least* one extra copy so that

   A. it can be sent to a newspaper
   B. there will be no mistakes made
   C. a personal record can be kept
   D. the information in the report can be discussed by all other security officers

13. In writing a report about a storeroom robbery by several men, the LEAST important of the following information is

    A. the number of men involved
    B. a list of the items that were stolen
    C. how the men entered the storeroom
    D. how many lights were left on by the robbers

Questions 14-19.

DIRECTIONS: Questions 14 to 19 are based on the paragraph REGISTRY SHEETS shown below. When answering these questions, refer to this paragraph.

REGISTRY SHEETS

Where registry sheets are in effect, the security officer must legibly print Authority employee's pass number, title, license and vehicle number, destination, time in and time out; and each Authority employee must sign his or her name. The same procedure is to be applied to visitors, except in place of a pass number each visitor will indicate his address or firm name; and visitors must also sign waivers. Information is to be obtained from driver's license, firm credential card, or any other appropriate identification, All visitors must state their purpose for entering upon the property. If they desire to visit anyone, verification must be made before entry is permitted. All persons signing sheet must sign in when entering upon the property, and sign out again when leaving. The security officer will, at the end of his tour, draw a horizontal line across the entire sheet after his last entry, indicating the end of one tour and the beginning of another. At the top of each sheet the security officer will enter the number of entries made during his tour, the sheet number, post, and date. Sheets are to begin with number 1 on the first day of the month, and should be kept in numerical order. Each security officer will read the orders at each post to see whether any changes are made and at which hours control sheets are in effect.

14. Waivers need NOT be signed by

    A. Authority employees   B. vendors
    C. reporters   D. salesmen

15. All visitors are required to state

    A. whether they have a criminal record
    B. the reason for their visit
    C. the reason they are not bonded
    D. whether they have ever worked for the Authority

16. In the paragraph, the statement is made that "verification must be made before entry is permitted." The word *verification* means, most nearly,

    A. allowance   B. confirmation   C. refusal   D. disposal

17. A security officer must draw a horizontal line across the entire registry sheet in order to show that

    A. he is being replaced to check a disturbance outside
    B. the last tour for the day has been completed
    C. one tour is ending and another is beginning
    D. a visitor has finished his business and is leaving

18. At the top of a registry sheet, it is NOT necessary for a security officer to list the

   A. tour number
   B. number of entries made
   C. sheet number
   D. date

19. A security officer should check at which hours control sheets are in effect by reading

   A. registry sheet number 1, on the first day of each month
   B. the orders at each post
   C. the time in and time out that each person has entered on the registry sheet
   D. the last entry made on the registry sheet used before the start of his tour

20. Assume that after working as a security officer for some time, your foreman is replaced by a new foreman.
   If this new foreman insists on explaining to you the procedure for doing a job which you know how to do very well, you should listen to the new foreman MAINLY because

   A. you may catch him in an error and thus prove you know your job
   B. it is wise to humor a foreman even when he is wrong
   C. you can do the job the way you like after the foreman leaves
   D. it will be your responsibility to perform the job the way the new foreman wants it done

21. All security officers are instructed that whenever they report an accident to the main office by telephone, prior to preparing their written accident report, they should request the name of the person receiving the call and also make a note of the time.
   The MAIN purpose of this precaution is to fix responsibility for the

   A. cause of the accident
   B. recording of the accident at the main office
   C. accuracy of the accident report
   D. preparation of the written report

22. One of your duties as a security officer will be to compile the facts about an accident in a written report. The LEAST important item to include in such an accident report is

   A. the people involved
   B. what action you took
   C. the extent of personal injuries
   D. why you think the accident happened

23. It is MOST important for a written report to be

   A. accurate
   B. brief
   C. detailed
   D. properly punctuated

24. In a large bus shop where many security officers are used, each security officer is required to do his work in a definite prescribed manner MAINLY because

   A. this practice insures discipline
   B. no other method will work
   C. this practice will keep the security officer from being inattentive on the job
   D. there will be less need for the security officers to consult with their supervisors

25. When an unusual situation arises on the job, and it would take too long for you to contact your foreman for advice, the *BEST* procedure for you to follow is to

    A. play it safe and take no action
    B. confer with another security officer
    C. check your rule book for the proper procedure
    D. act according to your best judgment

26. At the scene of an accident it is good first-aid procedure to treat the most badly injured person first. Of the following injured people, the person *LEAST* in need of immediate care is one who

    A. is bleeding rapidly
    B. finds great difficulty in breathing
    C. appears to have sprained an ankle
    D. complains of severe pains in his chest

Questions 27-32.

DIRECTIONS: Questions 27 to 32 are based on the paragraph THEFT shown below. When answering these questions, refer to this paragraph.

THEFT

A security officer must be alert at all times to discourage the willful removal of property and material of the Authority by individuals for self gain. Should a security officer detect such an individual, he should detain him and immediately call the supervisor at that location. No force should be used during the process of detainment. However, should the individual bolt from the premises, the security officer will be expected to offer some clues for his apprehension. Therefore, he should try to remember some characteristic traits about the individual, such as clothing, height, coloring, speech, and how he made his approach. Unusual characteristics such as a scar or a limp are most important. If a car is used, the security officer should take the license plate number of said car. Above information should be supplied to the responding peace officer and the special inspection control desk. In desolate locations, the security officer should first call the police and then the special inspection control desk. Any security officer having information of the theft should contact the director of special inspection by telephone or by mail. This information will be kept confidential if desired.

27. A security officer is required to be attentive on the job at all times, *MAINLY* to

    A. get as much work done as possible
    B. prevent the stealing of Authority property
    C. show his supervisor that he is doing a good job
    D. prevent any other security officer from patrolling the area to which he is assigned

28. In the second sentence, the word *detain* means, most nearly,

    A. delay   B. avoid   C. call   D. report

29. The prescribed course of action a security officer should take when he discovers a person stealing Authority property is to

    A. make sure that all gates are closed to prevent the thief from escaping
    B. detain the thief and quickly call the supervisor

C. use his club to keep the thief there until the police arrive
D. call another security officer for assistance

30. The MOST useful of the following descriptions of a runaway thief would be that he is a

A. tall man who runs fast
B. man with blue eyes
C. man with black hair
D. tall man who limps

31. The license plate number of a car which is used by a thief to escape should be reported by & security officer to the responding peace officer *and* the

A. director of protection agents
B. security officer's supervisor
C. special inspection control desk
D. department of motor vehicles

32. A security officer patrolling a desolate area has spotted a thief. The security officer should FIRST call

A. his supervisor
B. the police
C. the special inspection control desk
D. the director of special inspection

33. It is very important that Authority officials be given legible hand-written reports on unusual occurrences if there is no time to type them up.
According to the above statement about hand-written reports, it would be MOST useful if a security officer, when writing a report,

A. did not write on the back of the page
B. did not use big words
C. wrote concisely
D. wrote out all the information clearly

34. A security officer sees a youth marking up the wall surrounding Authority property. He should FIRST

A. tell the youth to stop
B. arrest the youth
C. call a policeman
D. punish the youth

35. If an alarm goes off and a security officer observes a van speeding away from a storeroom, the information that would be LEAST helpful in identifying the van would be the

A. color of the van
B. approximate speed at which the van passed his post
C. state and the license plate number of the van
D. manufacturer and model of the van

36. A security officer notices that a power line, knocked down by a storm, has electrified a steel flagpole. After notifying his supervisor, of the following it would be BEST to

A. put a wooden "caution" sign on the flagpole and call the Fire Department
B. remove the wire from the flagpole
C. stay near the flagpole and warn everyone not to go near the flagpole
D. say nothing about it until his supervisor arrives

37. Another Authority employee informs a security officer, who is on duty at the entrance to an Authority bus depot, that he has found a bomb in the locker room. The security officer should FIRST

   A. investigate to see if it is actually a bomb
   B. clear the area of persons in or near the locker room
   C. question the man closely to determine if he really saw a bomb
   D. call the Bomb Squad for instructions on handling bombs

38. In MOST cases, a written report on an accident is better than an oral report because a written report

   A. can be referred to later
   B. takes less time to prepare
   C. includes more of the facts
   D. reduces the number of court cases

39. A report of an accident is MOST likely to be accurate if written by the security officer

   A. long after the event
   B. after taking about a week to make sure he has all the facts
   C. immediately after the event
   D. after thoroughly discussing the event with others for several days

40. The gross weight of a carton and its contents is 830.2 pounds. If the weight of the carton alone is 98.7 pounds, the net weight of the contents of the carton is

   A. 731.5 pounds   B. 732.5 pounds
   C. 741.5 pounds   D. 831.5 pounds

KEY (CORRECT ANSWERS)

1. C	11. C	21. B	31. C
2. C	12. C	22. D	32. B
3. D	13. D	23. A	33. D
4. C	14. A	24. D	34. A
5. B	15. B	25. D	35. B
6. A	16. B	26. C	36. C
7. D	17. C	27. B	37. B
8. C	18. A	28. A	38. A
9. B	19. B	29. B	39. C
10. C	20. D	30. D	40. A

TEST 2

DIRECTIONS: Each question or incomplete statement is followed by several suggested answers or completions. Select the one that *BEST* answers the question or completes the statement. *PRINT THE LETTER OF THE CORRECT ANSWER TN THE SPACE AT THE RIGHT.*

Questions 1-10.

DIRECTIONS: Read the DESCRIPTION OF ACCIDENT carefully. Then answer Questions 1 to 10, inclusive, using only this information in picking your answer.

DESCRIPTION OF ACCIDENT

On Friday, May 9th, at about 2:30 p.m, Bus Operator Joe Able, badge no, 1234, was operating his half-filled bus, Authority no. 5678, northbound along Fifth Ave., when a green Ford truck, N.Y. license no. 9012, driven by Sam Wood, came out of an Authority storeroom entrance into the path of the bus. To avoid hitting the truck, Joe Able turned his steering wheel sharply to the left, causing his bus to cross the solid white line into the opposite lane where the bus crashed head-on into a black 1975 Mercury, N.Y. license no. 3456, driven by Bill Green. The crash caused the Mercury to sideswipe a blue VW, N.J. license 7890, driven by Jim White, which was double-parked while he made a delivery. The sudden movement of the bus caused one of the passengers, Mrs. Jane Smith, to fall, striking her head on one of the seats, Joe Able blew his horn vigorously to summon aid and Security Officer Fred Norton, badge no. 9876, and Stockman Al Blue, badge no. 5432, came out of the storeroom and rendered assistance. While Norton gave Mrs. Smith first aid, Blue summoned an ambulance for Green. A tow truck removed Green's car and Able found that the bus could operate under its own power, so he returned to the garage.

1. The Ford truck was driven by 1.____
   - A. Able
   - B. Green
   - C. Wood
   - D. White

2. The Authority no. of the bus was 2.____
   - A. 1234
   - B. 5678
   - C. 9012
   - D. 3456

3. The bus was driven by 3.____
   - A. Able
   - B. Green
   - C. Wood
   - D. White

4. The license no. of the VW was 4.____
   - A. 9012
   - B. 3456
   - C. 7890
   - D. 5432

5. The horn of the bus summoned 5.____
   - A. Blue
   - B. Green
   - C. White
   - D. Smith

6. The badge no. of the security officer was 6.____
   - A. 5432
   - B. 5678
   - C. 1234
   - D. 9876

7. The Mercury was driven by 7.____
   - A. Smith
   - B. Norton
   - C. White
   - D. Green

8. The bus was traveling

    A. North B. East C. South D. West

9. The vehicle towed away was a

    A. bus B. Ford C. Mercury D. VW

10. Mrs. Smith hurt her

    A. head B. back C. arm D. leg

11. If more than one security officer is involved in an incident, each is required to write a report giving his version of what happened. By having *both* reports submitted, the information gathered

    A. should be more complete
    B. should clear the Authority from any blame
    C. cannot be disputed
    D. will not be opinionated

12. If a security officer gets $5.42 per hour, and $8.13 per hour for overtime work, his *gross* salary for a week in which he works 5 hours over his regular 40 hours is

    A. $216.80 B. $243.90 C. $257.45 D. $325.20

13. It takes 2 min. 45 sec. for a security officer to travel to his first clock station, 3 min. to get to the second, 2 min. to get to the third, 5 1/2 min. to get to the fourth, and 4 min. 15 sec. to get from the fourth back to the starting point.
    Neglecting the time spent at each clock station, the *TOTAL* time needed to make one round tour is

    A. 16 min. 45 sec. B. 17 min. 15 sec.
    C. 17 min. 30 sec. D. 18 min.

Questions 14-20.

DIRECTIONS: Questions 14 to 20 are based on the rules listed below and are numbered 1 to 7. Each question gives a situation in which a security officer has disobeyed at least one rule. For each question, select from among the four choices the number of a rule which the security officer has disobeyed.

Rule Number 1: A security officer is subject to the orders of foremen (security officer) and of employees assigned to the special inspection control desk.

Rule Number 2: A security officer must protect system properties against fire, theft, vandalism, and unauthorized entrance.

Rule Number 3: A security officer is responsible for all equipment and other property entrusted to him and must see that such equipment is kept in good condition.

Rule Number 4: A security officer must give information about an accident only to authorized Authority officials.

Rule Number 5: A security officer must be attired in the prescribed uniform with badge displayed at all times while on duty.

Rule Number 6: A security officer must remain on duty during his entire tour and must therefore eat lunch on the job.

Rule Number 7: A security officer must not allow another employee to perform any part of his duties without proper authority.

14. While investigating a noise in the parking lot at night, Security Officer Johnson could not see very well because his flashlight was not in working order. Johnson disobeyed Rule Number

    A. 1 B. 3 C. 5 D. 7

14._____

15. Without getting permission to do so, Security Officer Simpson went to the locker room to get his lunch and let the porter, Baxter, check the credentials of a truck driver whose truck was about to enter Authority property. Simpson disobeyed Rule Number

    A. 1 B. 3 C. 5 D. 7

15._____

16. After being told by his foreman to check the door of Storeroom No. 15 before leaving, Security Officer Roscoe went off duty before seeing whether or not the door was properly locked. Roscoe disobeyed Rule Number

    A. 1 B. 4 C. 6 D. 7

16._____

17. Security Officer Andrews removed his badge ten minutes before going off duty. Andrews disobeyed Rule Number

    A. 2 B. 4 C. 5 D. 6

17._____

18. Security Officer Paul left his post inside the train yard in order to make a personal telephone call. As a result, Paul disobeyed Rule Number

    A. 2 B. 4 C. 5 D. 7

18._____

19. Security Officer Burroughs gave a newspaper reporter details of an accident that occurred on his post. Burroughs disobeyed Rule Number

    A. 1 B. 2 C. 3 D. 4

19._____

20. Security Officer Grenich left his post unattended and went across the street to a diner, since he left his lunch at home. Grenich disobeyed Rule Number

    A. 4 B. 5 C. 6 D. 7

20._____

Questions 21-25.

DIRECTIONS: Questions 21 to 25 are based on the UNUSUAL OCCURRENCE REPORT given below. Five phrases in the report have been removed and are listed below the report as 1. through 5. In each of the five places where phrases of the report have been left out, the number of a question has been inserted. For each question, select the number of the missing phrase which would make the report read correctly.

4 (#2)

UNUSUAL OCCURRENCE REPORT

Post 20A
Tour 12 a.m.-8 a.m.
Date August 13

Location of Occurrence: Storeroom #55

REMARKS: While making rounds this morning I thought that I heard some strange sounds coming from Storeroom #55. Upon investigation, I saw that 21 and that the door to the storeroom was slightly opened. At 2:45 a.m. I 22 .

Suddenly two men jumped out from 23 , dropped the tools which they were holding, and made a dash for the door. I ordered them to stop, but they just kept running.

I was able to get a good look at both of them. One man was wearing a green jacket and had a full beard and the other was short and had blond hair. Immediately, I called the police and about two minutes later I notified 24 . I 25 the police arrived and I gave them the complete details of the incident.

Security Officer Donald Rimson 23807
Signature Pass No.

1. the special inspection control desk
2. behind some crates
3. the lock had been tampered with
4. remained at the storeroom until
5. entered the storeroom and began to look around

21. A. 1   B. 3   C. 4   D. 5   21.____
22. A. 2   B. 3   C. 4   D. 5   22.____
23. A. 1   B. 2   C. 3   D. 4   23.____
24. A. 1   B. 2   C. 3   D. 4   24.____
25. A. 2   B. 3   C. 4   D. 5   25.____

26. Employees using supplies from a first-aid kit are generally required to submit an immediate report on what happened and what supplies were used. 26.____
    Of the following, the MOST important reason for this regulation is to

    A. make sure that supplies which are used are replaced
    B. prevent theft
    C. see that the correct employee gets credit for taking action
    D. identify the person who last used the kit

27. The log book of a security officer stationed at an entry gate shows 47 entries in two hours. At this rate, the number of entries in eight hours is 27.____

    A. 108   B. 168   C. 188   D. 376

28. A truck driver leaving Authority property has a requisition form showing 14 cartons of pencils, 12 cartons of pens, 27 cartons of envelopes, and 39 cartons of writing pads. If an actual count of the cartons on the truck shows only 77 cartons, the number of cartons missing is 28.____

    A. 15   B. 14   C. 12   D. 5

29. It is *NOT* advisable to move an injured man before the arrival of a doctor if the man has

    A. a severe nosebleed
    B. burns over 3% of his body
    C. fainted from the heat
    D. possibly injured his spine

30. While making rounds during daylight hours, a security officer notices that one of the floodlights in the parking lot has been left on. The security officer should

    A. turn the light off because it will cost him his job if his foreman finds out about this
    B. turn the light off, because it is not needed
    C. leave the light on and call his foreman to investigate
    D. leave the light on to make it easier for him to see anything which looks suspicious

31. A security officer comes upon an empty fire extinguisher while making his rounds. Of the following, it is *MOST* important that he

    A. ignore it, since mentioning this might get someone into trouble
    B. make a note not to use that extinguisher in case of a fire
    C. report it to the next security officer who relieves him
    D. report it to his foreman

32. The windows of the booth used by a security officer must be kept clean and clear of any obstructions at all times. The *MOST* obvious reason for this is to

    A. enable anyone passing by the booth to look into it and see who is on duty
    B. allow as much daylight as possible to enter the booth so that a security officer can conserve electricity by keeping booth lights turned off
    C. enable a security officer to see what is happening outside of the booth
    D. make certain that a security officer makes a good impression on inspectors who are passing by the booth

33. A security officer must be completely familiar with door schedules (when the door must be locked and when open), particularly during hours when employees are reporting for work.
    If a security officer does not know all door schedules for his post it would be *BEST* for him to

    A. quickly get a copy of the door schedule from the security officer who will relieve him
    B. check the bulletin board at a nearby post to see if he can get a copy of the door schedules
    C. let his foreman know about it immediately, so the foreman can give him the information he needs
    D. check the rules and regulations book for the information

Questions 34-37.

DIRECTIONS: Questions 34 to 37 inclusive are based on the paragraph FIRE FIGHTING shown below. When answering these questions, refer to this paragraph.

FIRE FIGHTING

A security officer should remember the cardinal rule that water or soda acid fire extinguishers should not be used on any electrical fire, and apply it in the case of a fire near the third rail. In addition, security officers should familiarize themselves with all available fire alarms and fire-fighting equipment within their assigned posts. Use of the fire alarm should bring responding Fire Department apparatus quickly to the scene. Familiarity with the fire-fighting equipment near his post would help in putting out incipient fires. Any man calling for the Fire Department should remain outside so that he can direct the Fire Department to the fire. As soon as possible thereafter, the special inspection desk must be notified and a complete written report of the fire, no matter how small, must be submitted to this office. The security officer must give the exact time and place it started, who discovered it, how it was extinguished, the damage done, cause of same, list of any injured persons with the extent of their injuries, and the name of the Fire Chief in charge. All defects noticed by the security officer concerning the fire alarm or any firefighting equipment must be reported to the special inspection department.

34. It would be proper to use water to put out a fire in a(n)

    A. electric motor
    B. electric switch box
    C. waste paper trash can
    D. electric generator

35. After calling the Fire Department from a street box to report a fire, the security officer should then

    A. return to the fire and help put it out
    B. stay outside and direct the Fire Department to the fire
    C. find a phone and call his boss
    D. write out a report for the special inspection desk

36. A security officer is required to submit a complete written report of a fire

    A. two weeks after the fire
    B. the day following the fire
    C. as soon as possible
    D. at his convenience

37. In his report of a fire, it is NOT necessary for the security officer to state

    A. time and place of the fire
    B. who discovered the fire
    C. the names of persons injured
    D. quantity of Fire Department equipment used

38. While making afternoon rounds, a security officer climbs a stairway which has a loose banister.
    To avoid having someone injured, the security officer should

    A. inform his foreman of the hazard so that it can be corrected
    B. fix the banister himself, since it can probably be fixed quickly
    C. block the stairway with rope at the top and bottom so that no one else can use it
    D. put up a caution sign in the hallway leading to the stairway

39. If, while on duty, a security officer sees an accident which results in injuries to Authority employees, it would be most important for him to FIRST

    A. render all possible first-aid to the injured
    B. record the exact time the accident happened
    C. write out an accident report
    D. try to find out what caused the accident

40. If a security officer has many accidents, no matter what shift or location he is assigned to, the MOST likely reason for this is

    A. lack of safety devices
    B. not enough safety posters
    C. inferior equipment and materials
    D. careless work practices

KEY (CORRECT ANSWERS)

1. C	11. A	21. B	31. D
2. B	12. C	22. D	32. C
3. A	13. C	23. B	33. C
4. C	14. B	24. A	34. C
5. A	15. D	25. C	35. B
6. D	16. A	26. A	36. C
7. D	17. C	27. C	37. D
8. A	18. A	28. A	38. A
9. C	19. D	29. D	39. A
10. A	20. C	30. B	40. D

EXAMINATION SECTION
TEST 1

DIRECTIONS: Questions 1 through 5 are to be answered on the basis of the information, instructions, and sample question given below. Each question contains a GENERAL RULE, EXCEPTIONS, a PROBLEM, and the ACTION actually taken.

The GENERAL RULE explains what the special officer (security officer) should or should not do.

The EXCEPTIONS describe circumstances under which a special officer (security officer) should take action contrary to the GENERAL RULE.

However, an unusual emergency may justify taking an action that is not covered either by the GENERAL RULE or by the stated EXCEPTIONS.

The PROBLEM describes a situation requiring some action by the special officer (security officer).

ACTION describes what a special officer (security officer) actually did in that particular case.

Read carefully the GENERAL RULE and EXCEPTIONS, the PROBLEM, and the ACTION, and the mark A, B, C, or D in the space at the right in accordance with the following instructions:

    I.   If an action is clearly justified under the general rule, mark your answer A.
    II. If an action is not justified under the general rule, but is justified under a stated exception, mark your answer B.
    III. If an action is not justified either by the general rule or by a stated exception, but does seem strongly justified by an unusual emergency situation, mark your answer C.
    IV. If an action does not seem justified for any of these reasons, mark your answer D.

SAMPLE QUESTION:

GENERAL RULE: A special officer (security officer) is not empowered to stop a person and search him for hidden weapons.
EXCEPTION: He may stop a person and search him if he has good reason to believe that he may be carrying a hidden weapon. Good reasons to believe he may be carrying a hidden weapon include (a) notification through official channels that a person may be armed, (b) a statement directly to the special officer (security officer) by the person himself that he is armed, and (c) the special officer's (security officer's) own direct observation.

PROBLEM: A special officer (security officer) on duty at a hospital clinic is notified by a woman patient at the clinic that a man sitting near her is making muttered threats that he has a gun and is going to shoot his doctor if the doctor gives him any trouble. Although the woman is upset, she seems to be telling the truth, and two other waiting patients con-

firm this. However, the special officer (security officer) approaches the man and sees no sign of a hidden weapon. The man tells the officer that he has no weapon.
ACTION: The special officer (security officer) takes the man aside into an empty office and proceeds to frisk him for a concealed weapon.

ANSWER: The answer cannot be A, because the general rule is that a special officer (security officer) is not empowered to search a person for hidden weapons. The answer cannot be B, because the notification did not come through official channels, the man did not tell the special officer (security officer) that he had a weapon, and the special officer (security officer) did not observe any weapon. However, since three people have confirmed that the man has said he has a weapon and is threatening to use it, this is pretty clearly an emergency situation that calls for action. Therefore, the answer is C.

1. GENERAL RULE: A special officer (security officer) on duty at a certain entrance is not to leave his post unguarded at any time.
   EXCEPTION: He may leave the post for a brief period if he first summons a replacement. He may also leave if it is necessary for him to take prompt emergency action to prevent injury to persons or property.
   PROBLEM: The special officer (security officer) sees a man running down a hall with a piece of iron pipe in his hand, chasing another man who is shouting for help. By going in immediate pursuit, there is a good chance that the special officer (security officer) can stop the man with the pipe.
   ACTION: The special officer (security officer) leaves his post unguarded and pursues the man.

   The CORRECT answer is:

   A. I   B. II   C. III   D. IV

2. GENERAL RULE: Special officers (security officers) assigned to a college campus are instructed not to arrest students for minor violations such as disorderly conduct; instead, the violation should be stopped and the incident should be reported to the college authorities, who will take disciplinary action.
   EXCEPTION: A special officer (security officer) may arrest a student or take other appropriate action if failure to do so is likely to result in personal injury or property damage, or disruption of school activities, or if the incident involves serious criminal behavior.
   PROBLEM: A special officer (security officer) is on duty in a college building where evening classes are being held. He is told that two students are causing a disturbance in a classroom. He arrives and finds that a fist fight is in progress and the classroom is in an uproar. The special officer (security officer) separates the two students who are fighting and takes them out of the room. Both of them seem to be intoxicated. They both have valid student ID cards.
   ACTION: The special officer (security officer) takes down their names and addresses for his report, then tells them to leave the building with a warning not to return this evening.

   The CORRECT answer is:

   A. I   B. II   C. III   D. IV

3. GENERAL RULE: A special officer (security officer) is not permitted to carry a gun while on duty.
EXCEPTION: A special officer (security officer) who disarms a person must keep the weapon in his possession for the brief period before he can turn it over to the proper authorities. A special officer (security officer) who is NOT on duty may, like any other citizen, own and carry a gun if he has a proper permit from the Police Department.
PROBLEM: A special officer (security officer) is assigned to a post where there have been a series of violent incidents in the past few days. He feels that these incidents could have been controlled much more easily if the people involved had seen that the special officer (security officer) had a gun. He has a gun at home, for which he has a valid permit.
ACTION: The special officer (security officer) brings his gun when he goes on duty. He does not plan to use it, but just show people that he has it so that they will not start any trouble.

The CORRECT answer is:

A. I B. II C. III D. IV

4. GENERAL RULE: No one except a licensed physician or someone acting directly under a physician's orders may legally administer medicine to another person.
EXCEPTION: In a first aid situation, the special officer (security officer) is allowed to help a person suffering frori a heart condition or other disease to take medicine which the person has in his possession, provided that the person is conscious and requests this assistance.
PROBLEM: A special officer (security officer) on duty at a public building is told that a man has collapsed in the elevator. When the special officer (security officer) arrives at the scene, the man is barely conscious. He cannot speak, but he points to his pocket. The special officer (security officer) finds a pill bottle that says *one capsule in ease of need*. The man nods.
ACTION: The special officer (security officer) puts one capsule in the man's hand and guides the man's hand to his mouth.

The CORRECT answer is:

A. I B. II C. III D. IV

5. GENERAL RULE: In case of a fire drill or fire alarm, special officers (security officers) on patrol in a building are to remain in their assigned areas to assist in the evacuation of persons from the building and to make sure that no one takes advantage of the situation by stealing property that is left unguarded.
EXCEPTION: Should there be an actual fire, special officers (security officers) will follow whatever instructions are given by the firefighters or police officers who arrive on the scene to take charge.
PROBLEM: A special officer (security officer) is on duty patroling the fifth floor of a building when a fire alarm sounds. The fire is in a supply closet at one end of the fifth floor. All personnel have been evacuated from the floor. Neither police nor firemen have yet shown up.
ACTION: The special officer (security officer) stays on the fifth floor at a safe distance from the supply closet.

The CORRECT answer is:

A. I B. II C. III D. IV

KEY (CORRECT ANSWERS)

1. B
2. A
3. D
4. B
5. A

———

MAP READING

EXAMINATION SECTION
TEST 1

DIRECTIONS: Each question or incomplete statement is followed by several suggested answers or completions. Select the one that BEST answers the question or completes the statement. *PRINT THE LETTER OF THE CORRECT ANSWER IN THE SPACE AT THE RIGHT.*

Questions 1-3.

DIRECTIONS: Questions 1 through 3 are to be answered SOLELY on the basis of the map which appears on the next page. The flow of traffic is indicated by the arrow. If there is only one arrow shown, then traffic flows only in the direction indicated by the arrow. If there are two arrows shown, then traffic flows in both directions. You must follow the flow of traffic.

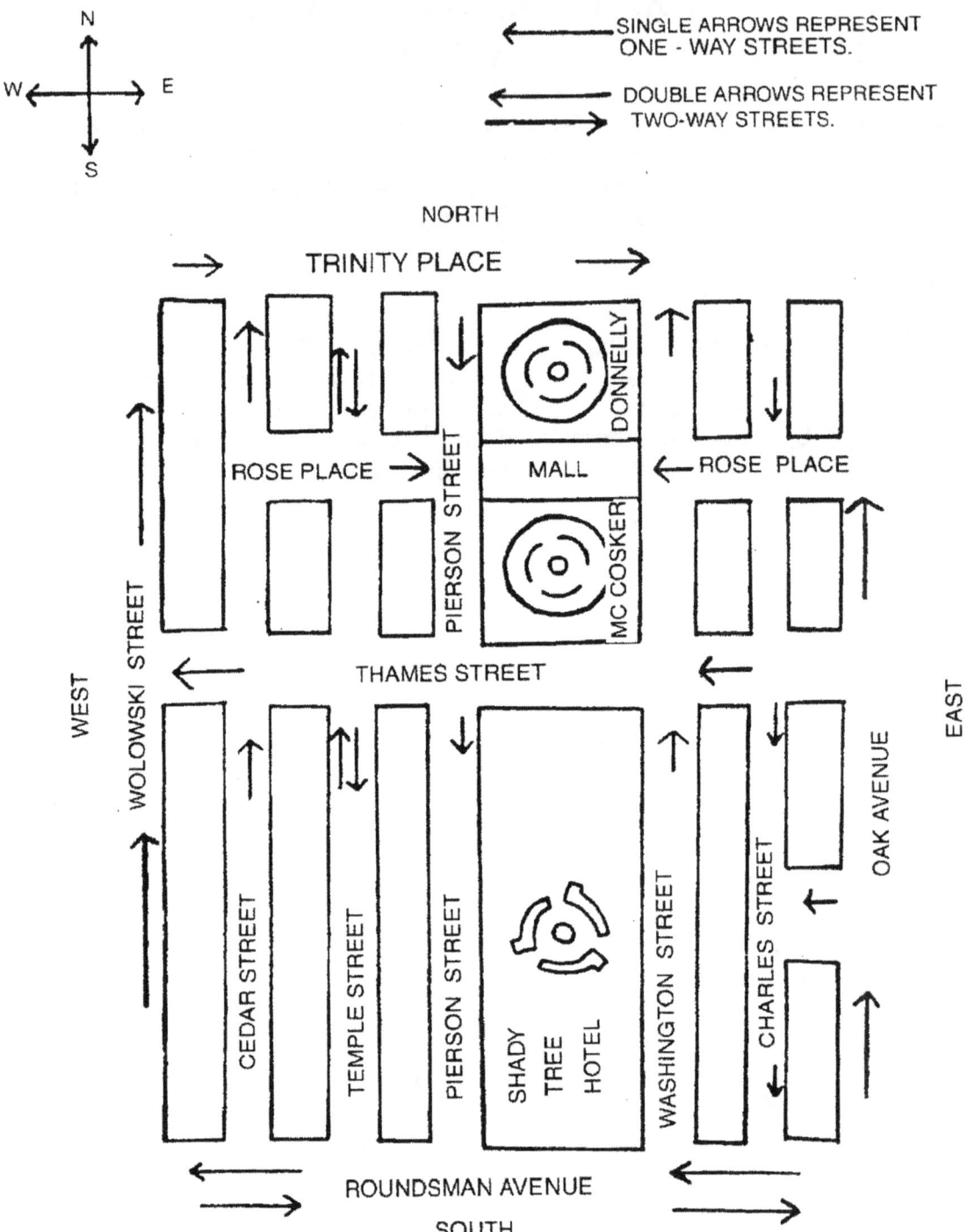

1. Police Officers Simms and O'Brien are located at Roundsman Avenue and Washington Street. The radio dispatcher has assigned them to investigate a motor vehicle accident at the corner of Pierson Street and Rose Place.
   Which one of the following is the SHORTEST route for them to take in their patrol car, making sure to obey all traffic regulations?
   Travel

   A. west on Roundsman Avenue, then north on Temple Street, then east on Thames Street, then north on Pierson Street to Rose Place
   B. east on Roundsman Avenue, then north on Oak Avenue, then west on Rose Place to Pierson Street
   C. west on Roundsman Avenue, then north on Temple Street, then east on Rose Place to Pierson Street
   D. east on Roundsman Avenue, then north on Oak Avenue, then west on Thames Street, then north on Temple Street, then east on Rose Place to Pierson Street

2. Police Officers Sears and Castro are located at Cedar Street and Roundsman Avenue. They are called to respond to the scene of a burglary at Rose Place and Charles Street. Which one of the following is the SHORTEST route for them to take in their patrol car, making sure to obey all traffic regulations?
   Travel

   A. east on Roundsman Avenue, then north on Oak Avenue, then west on Rose Place to Charles Street
   B. east on Roundsman Avenue, then north on Washington Street, then east on Rose Place to Charles Street
   C. west on Roundsman Avenue, then north on Wolowski Street, then east on Trinity Place, then south on Charles Street to Rose Place
   D. east on Roundsman Avenue, then north on Charles Street to Rose Place

3. Police Officer Glasser is in an unmarked car at the intersection of Rose Place and Temple Street when he begins to follow two robbery suspects. The suspects go south for two blocks, then turn left for two blocks, then make another left turn for one more block. The suspects realize they are being followed and make a left turn and travel two more blocks and then make a right turn.
   In what direction are the suspects now headed?

   A. North   B. South   C. East   D. West

Questions 4-6.

DIRECTIONS: Questions 4 through 6 are to be answered SOLELY on the basis of the following map. The flow of traffic is indicated by the arrows. If there is only one arrow shown, then traffic flows only in the direction indicated by the arrow. If there are two arrows shown, then traffic flows in both directions. You must follow the flow of traffic.

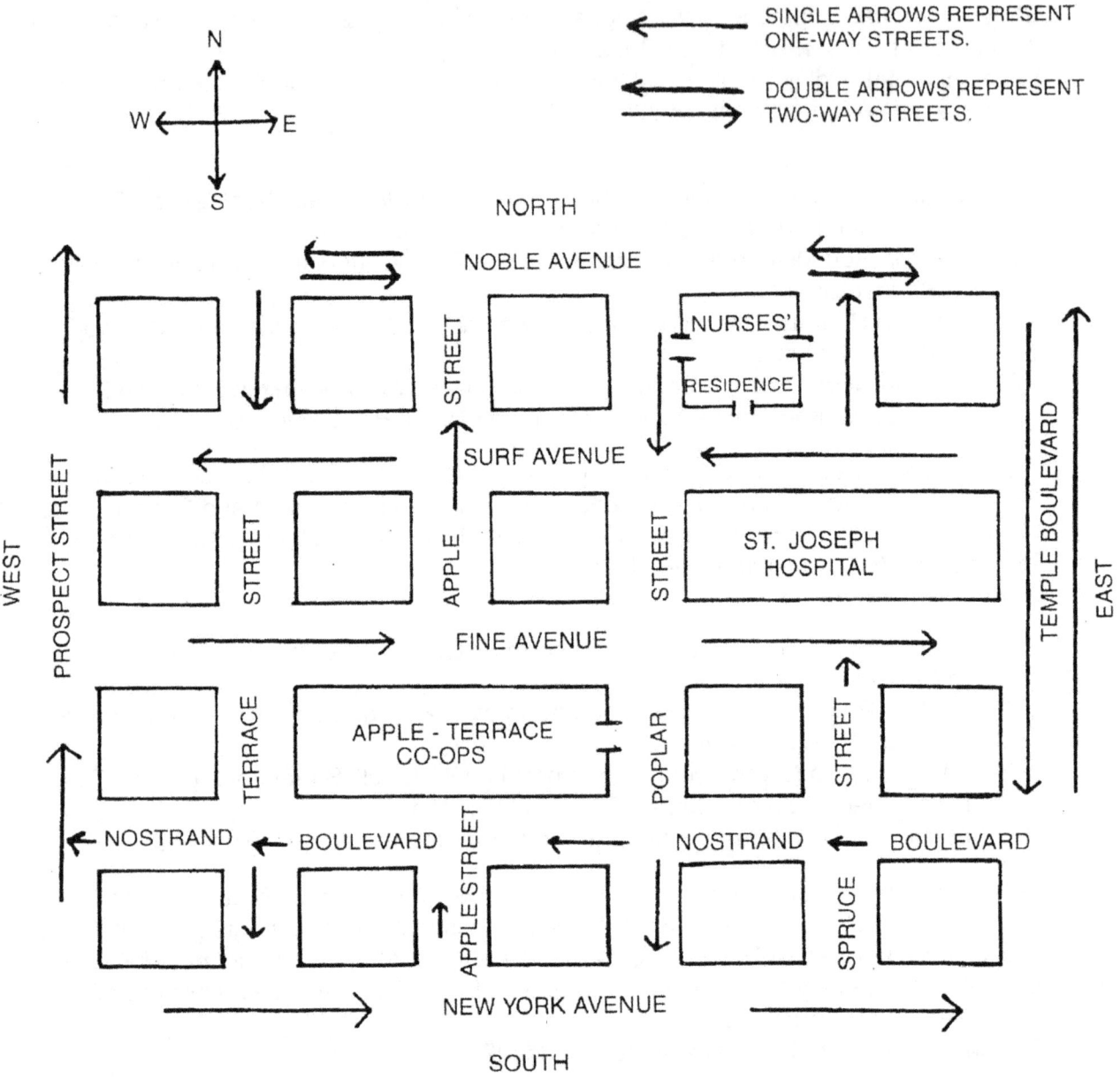

4. Police Officers Gannon and Vine are located at the intersection of Terrace Street and Surf Avenue when they receive a call from the radio dispatcher stating that they need to respond to an attempted murder at Spruce Street and Fine Avenue.
Which one of the following is the SHORTEST route for them to take in their patrol car, making sure to obey all traffic regulations?
Travel _____ to Spruce Street.

- A. west on Surf Avenue, then north on Prospect Street, then east on Noble Avenue, then south on Poplar Street, then east on Fine Avenue
- B. east on Surf Avenue, then south on Poplar Street, then east on Fine Avenue
- C. west on Surf Avenue, then south on Prospect Street, then east on Fine Avenue
- D. south on Terrace Street, then east on Fine Avenue

5. Police Officers Sears and Ronald are at Nostrand Boulevard and Prospect Street. They receive a call assigning them to investigate a disruptive group of youths at Temple Boulevard and Surf Avenue.
Which one of the following is the SHORTEST route for them to take in their patrol car, making sure to obey all traffic regulations?
Travel

   A. north on Prospect Street, then east on Surf Avenue to Temple Boulevard
   B. north on Prospect Street, then east on Noble Avenue, then south on Temple Boulevard to Surf Avenue
   C. north on Prospect Street, then east on Fine Avenue, then north on Temple Boulevard to Surf Avenue
   D. south on Prospect Street, then east on New York Avenue, then north on Temple Boulevard to Surf Avenue

5._____

6. While on patrol at Prospect Street and New York Avenue, Police Officers Ross and Rock are called to a burglary in progress near the entrance to the Apple-Terrace Co-ops on Poplar Street midway between Fine Avenue and Nostrand Boulevard.
Which one of the following is the SHORTEST route for them to take in their patrol car, making sure to obey all traffic regulations?
Travel _____ Poplar Street.

   A. east on New York Avenue, then north
   B. north on Prospect Avenue, then east on Fine Avenue, then south
   C. north on Prospect Street, then east on Surf Avenue, then south
   D. east on New York Avenue, then north on Temple Boulevard, then west on Surf Avenue, then south

6._____

Questions 7-8.

DIRECTIONS: Questions 7 and 8 are to be answered SOLELY on the basis of the map which appears below. The flow of traffic is indicated by the arrows. If there is only one arrow shown, then traffic flows only in the direction indicated by the arrow. If there are two arrows shown, then traffic flows in both directions. You must follow the flow of traffic.

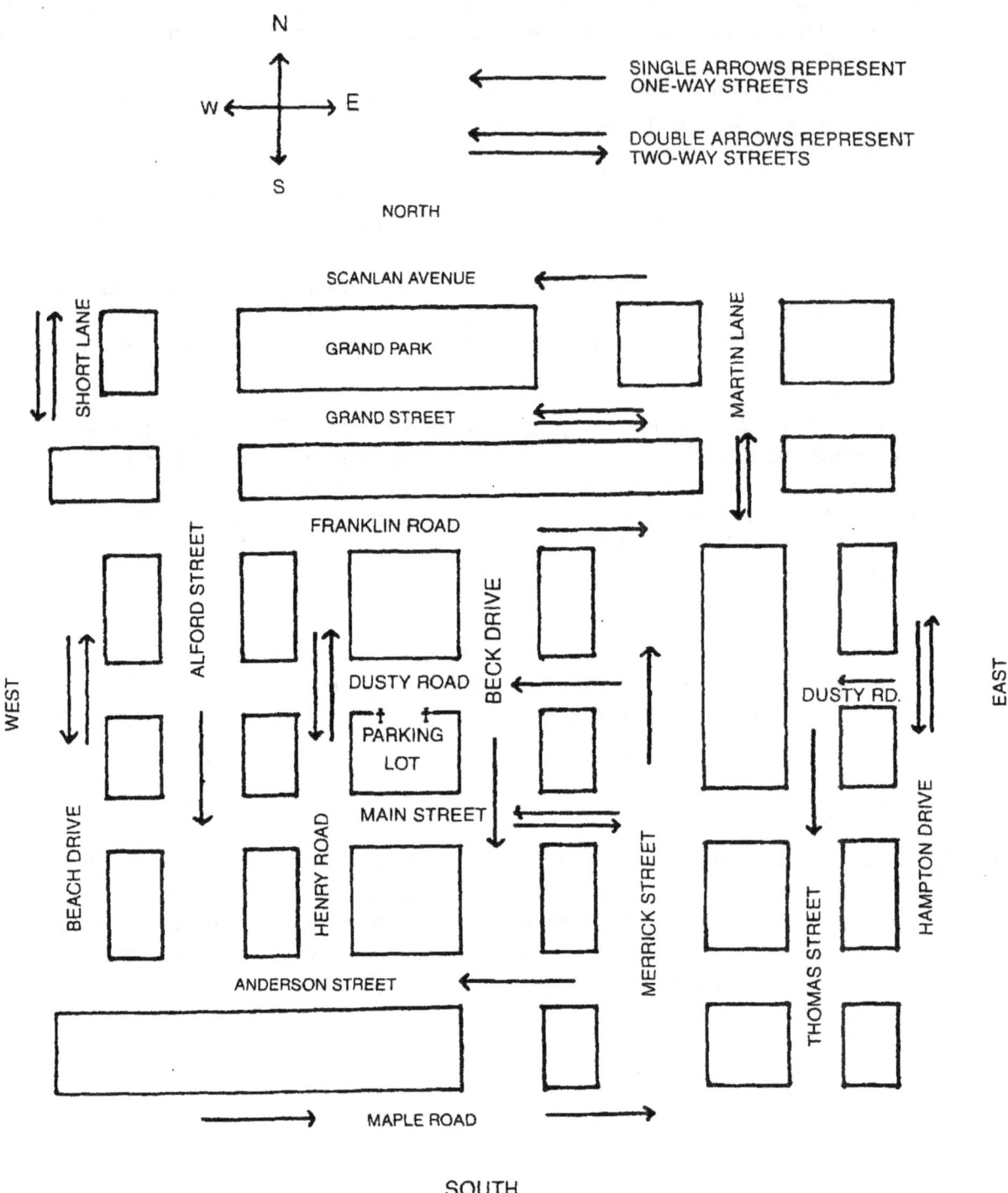

7. Police Officers Gold and Warren are at the intersection of Maple Road and Hampton Drive. The radio dispatcher has assigned them to investigate an attempted auto theft in the parking lot on Dusty Road.
Which one of the following is the SHORTEST route for the officers to take in their patrol car to get to the entrance of the parking lot on Dusty Road, making sure to obey all traffic regulations?
Travel _____ to the parking lot entrance.

7.___

A. north on Hampton Drive, then west on Dusty Road
B. west on Maple Road, then north on Beck Drive, then west on Dusty Road
C. north on Hampton Drive, then west on Anderson Street, then north on Merrick Street, then west on Dusty Road
D. west on Maple Road, then north on Merrick Street, then west on Dusty Road

8. Police Officer Gladden is in a patrol car at the intersection of Beach Drive and Anderson Street when he spots a suspicious car. Police Officer Gladden calls the radio dispatcher to determine if the vehicle was stolen. Police Officer Gladden then follows the vehicle north on Beach Drive for three blocks, then turns right and proceeds for one block and makes another right. He then follows the vehicle for two blocks, and then they both make a left turn and continue driving. Police Officer Gladden now receives a call from the dispatcher stating the car was reported stolen and signals for the vehicle to pull to the side of the road.
In what direction was Police Officer Gladden heading at the time he signaled for the other car to pull over?   8._____

A. North   B. East   C. South   D. West

Questions 9-10.

DIRECTIONS: Questions 9 and 10 are to be answered SOLELY on the basis of the map which appears on the following page. The flow of traffic is indicated by the arrows. If there is only one arrow shown, then traffic flows only in the direction indicated by the arrow. If there are two arrows shown, then traffic flows in both directions. You must follow the flow of traffic.

8 (#1)

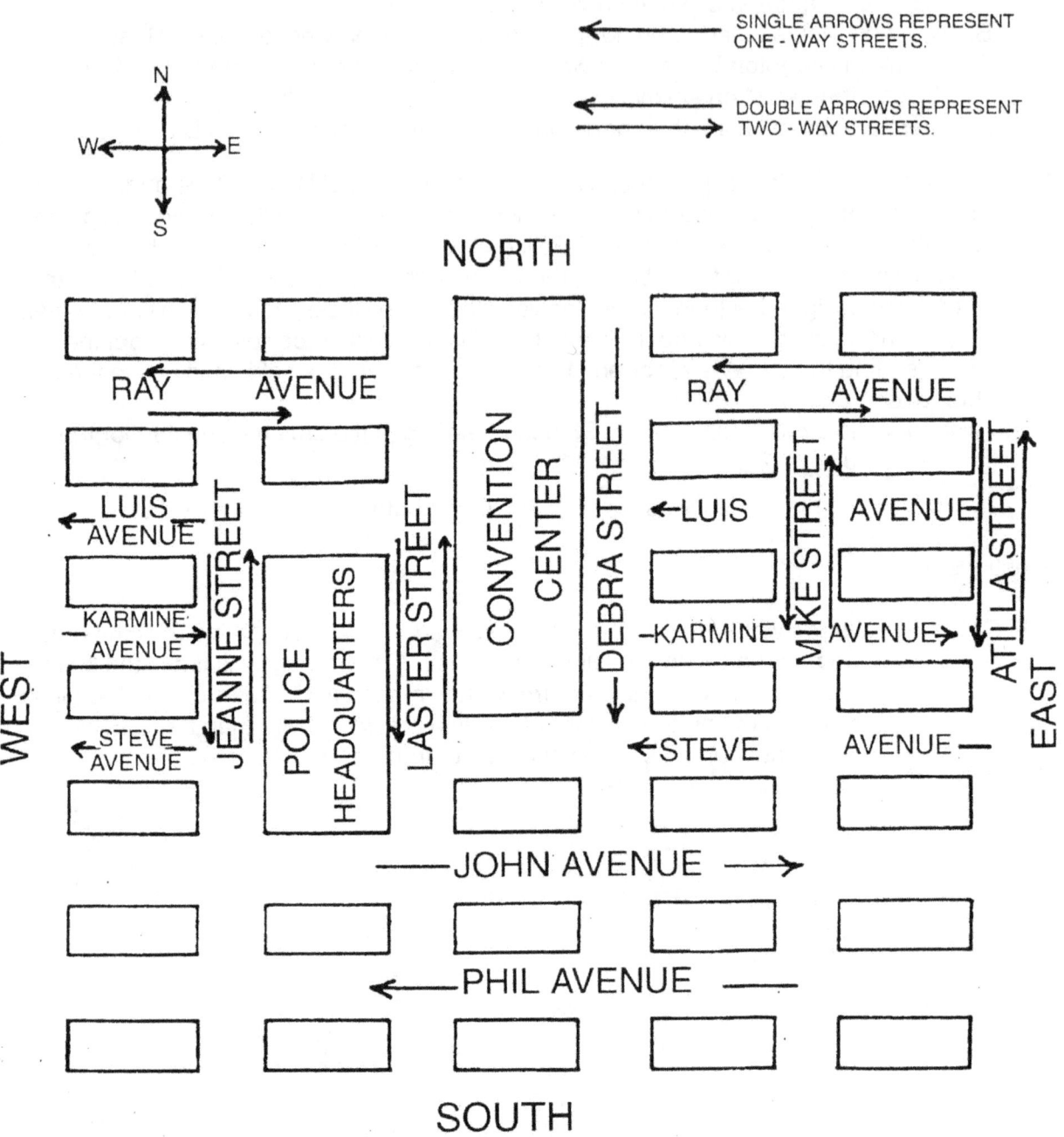

9. While in a patrol car located at Ray Avenue and Atilla Street, Police Officer Ashley receives a call from the dispatcher to respond to an assault at Jeanne Street and Karmine Avenue.
Which one of the following is the SHORTEST route for Officer Ashley to follow in his patrol car, making sure to obey all traffic regulations?
Travel

   A. south on Atilla Street, west on Luis Avenue, south on Debra Street, west on Steve Avenue, north on Lester Street, west on Luis Avenue, then one block south on Jeanne Street
   B. south on Atilla Street, then four blocks west on Phil Avenue, then north on Jeanne Street to Karmine Avenue

C. west on Ray Avenue to Debra Street, then five blocks south to Phil Avenue, then west to Jeanne Street, then three blocks north to Karmine Avenue
D. south on Atilla Street, then four blocks west on John Avenue, then north on Jeanne Street to Karmine Avenue

10. After taking a complaint report from the assault victim, Officer Ashley receives a call from the dispatcher to respond to an auto larceny in progress at the corner of Debra Street and Luis Avenue.
Which one of the following is the SHORTEST route for Officer Ashley to follow in his patrol car, making sure to obey all traffic regulations?
Travel

10._____

A. south on Jeanne Street to John Avenue, then east three blocks on John Avenue, then north on Mike Street to Luis Avenue, then west to Debra Street
B. south on Jeanne Street to John Avenue, then east two blocks on John Avenue, then north on Debra Street to Luis Avenue
C. north on Jeanne Street two blocks, then east on Ray Avenue for one block, then south on Lester Street to Steve Avenue, then one block east on Steve Avenue, then north on Debra Street to Luis Avenue
D. south on Jeanne Street to John Avenue, then east on John Avenue to Atilla Street, then north three blocks to Luis Avenue, then west to Debra Street

Questions 11-13.

DIRECTIONS: Questions 11 through 13 are to be answered SOLELY on the basis of the following map. The flow of traffic is indicated by the arrows. You must follow the flow of traffic.

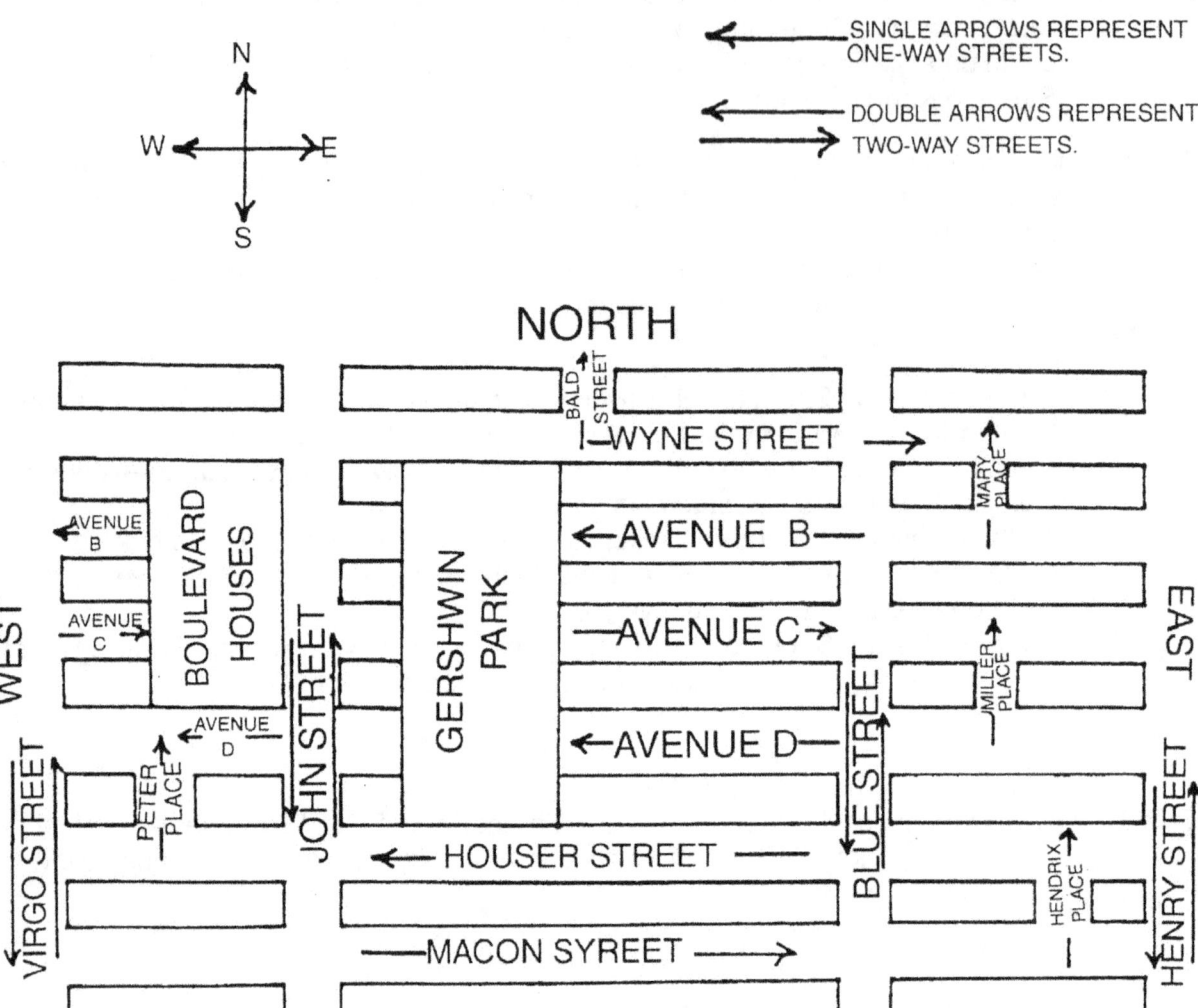

11. Police Officers Ranking and Fish are located at Wyne Street and John Street. The radio dispatcher has assigned them to investigate a motor vehicle accident at the corner of Henry Street and Houser Street.
Which one of the following is the SHORTEST route for them to take in their patrol car, making sure to obey all traffic regulations?
Travel

   A. four blocks south on John Street, then three blocks east on Houser Street to Henry Street
   B. two blocks east on Wyne Street, then two blocks south on Blue Street, then two blocks east on Avenue C, then two blocks south on Henry Street
   C. two blocks east on Wyne Street, then five blocks south on Blue Street, then two blocks east on Macon Street, then one block north on Henry Street
   D. five blocks south on John Street, then three blocks east on Macon Street, then one block north to Houser Street

12. Police Officers Rizzo and Latimer are located at Avenue B and Virgo Street. They respond to the scene of a robbery at Miller Place and Avenue D.
Which one of the following is the SHORTEST route for them to take in their patrol car, making sure to obey all traffic regulations?
Travel _____ to Miller Place.

    A. one block north on Virgo Street, then four blocks east on Wyne Street, then three blocks south on Henry Street, then one block west on Avenue D
    B. four blocks south on Virgo Street, then two blocks east on Macon Street, then two blocks north on Blue Street, then one block east on Avenue D
    C. three blocks south on Virgo Street, then east on Houser Street to Henry Street, then one block north on Henry Street, then one block west on Avenue D
    D. four blocks south on Virgo Street, then four blocks east to Henry Street, then north to Avenue D, then one block west

12.____

13. Police Officer Bendix is in an unmarked patrol car at the intersection of John Street and Macon Street when he begins to follow a robbery suspect. The suspect goes one block east, turns left, travels for three blocks, and then turns right. He drives for two blocks and then makes a right turn. In the middle of the block, the suspect realizes he is being followed and makes a u-turn. In what direction is the suspect now headed?

    A. North   B. South   C. East   D. West

13.____

Questions 14-15.

DIRECTIONS: Questions 14 and 15 are to be answered SOLELY on the basis of the following map. The flow of traffic is indicated by the arrows. If there is only one arrow shown, then traffic flows only in the direction indicated by the arrow. If there are two arrows shown, then traffic flows in both directions. You must follow the flow of traffic.

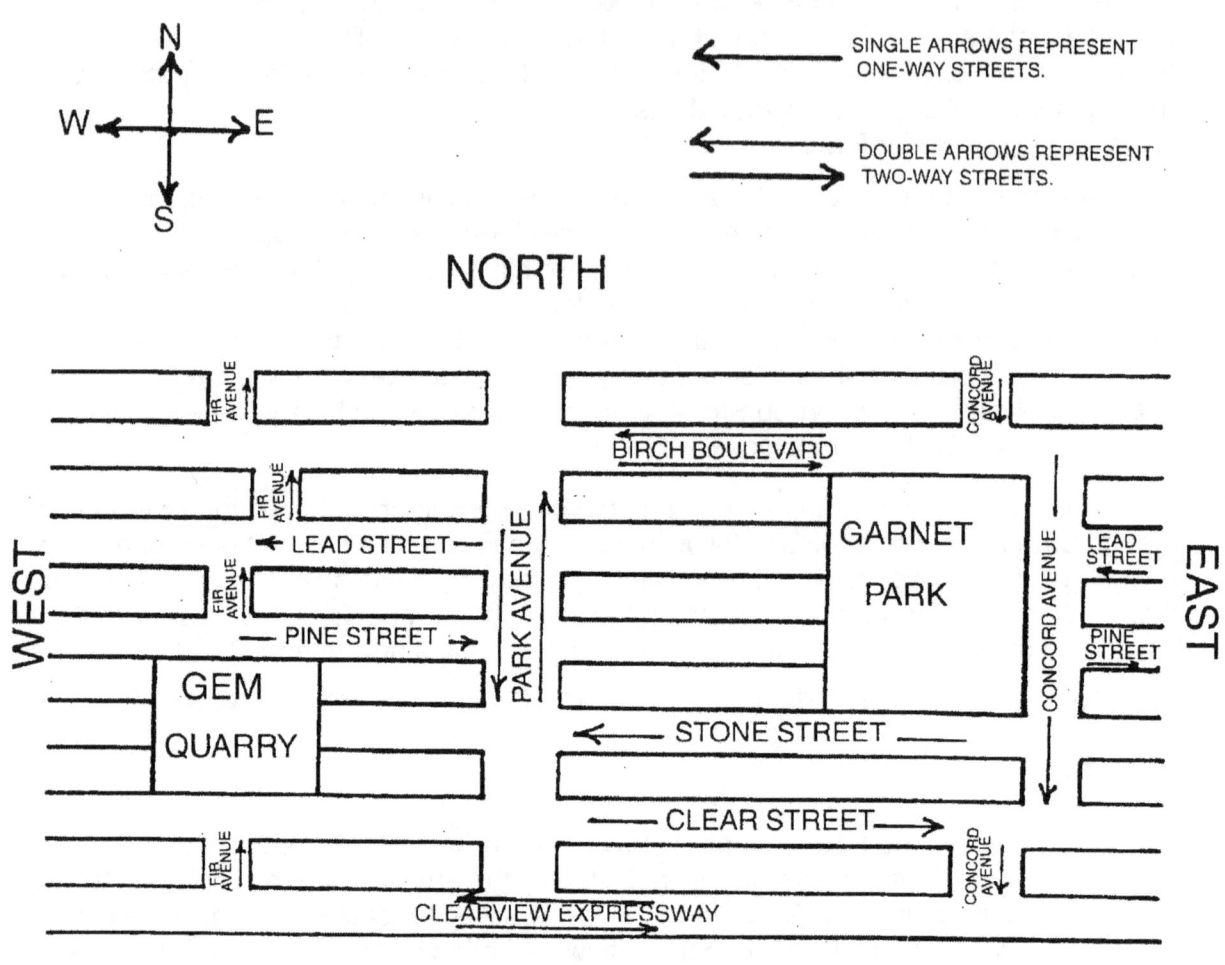

14. You are located at Fir Avenue and Birch Boulevard and receive a request to respond to a disturbance at Fir Avenue and Clear Street.
Which one of the following is the MOST direct route for you to take in your patrol car, making sure to obey all traffic regulations?
Travel

    A. one block east on Birch Boulevard, then four blocks south on Park Avenue, then one block east on Clear Street
    B. two blocks east on Birch Boulevard, then three blocks south on Concord Avenue, then two blocks west on Stone Street, then one block south on Park Avenue, then one block west on Clear Street
    C. one block east on Birch Boulevard, then five blocks south on Park Avenue, then one block west on the Clearview Expressway, then one block north on Fir Avenue
    D. two blocks south on Fir Avenue, then one block east on Pine Street, then three blocks south on Park Avenue, then one block east on the Clearview Expressway, then one block north on Fir Avenue

15. You are located at the Clearview Expressway and Concord Avenue and receive a call to respond to a crime in progress at Concord Avenue and Pine Street. Which one of the following is the MOST direct route for you to take in your patrol car, making sure to obey all traffic regulations?
Travel

    A. two blocks west on the Clearview Expressway, then one block north on Fir Avenue, then one block east on Clear Street, then four blocks north on Park Avenue, then one block east on Birch Boulevard, then two blocks south on Concord Avenue
    B. one block north on Concord Avenue, then one block west on Clear Street, then one block north on Park Avenue, then one block east on Stone Street, then one block north on Concord Avenue
    C. one block west on the Clearview Expressway, then four blocks north on Park Avenue, then one block west on Lead Street, then one block south on Fir Avenue
    D. one block west on the Clearview Expressway, then five blocks north on Park Avenue, then one block east on Birch Boulevard, then two blocks south on Concord Avenue

15.____

Questions 16-20.

DIRECTIONS: Questions 16 through 20 are to be answered SOLELY on the basis of the following map. The flow of traffic is indicated by the arrows. You must follow the flow of traffic.

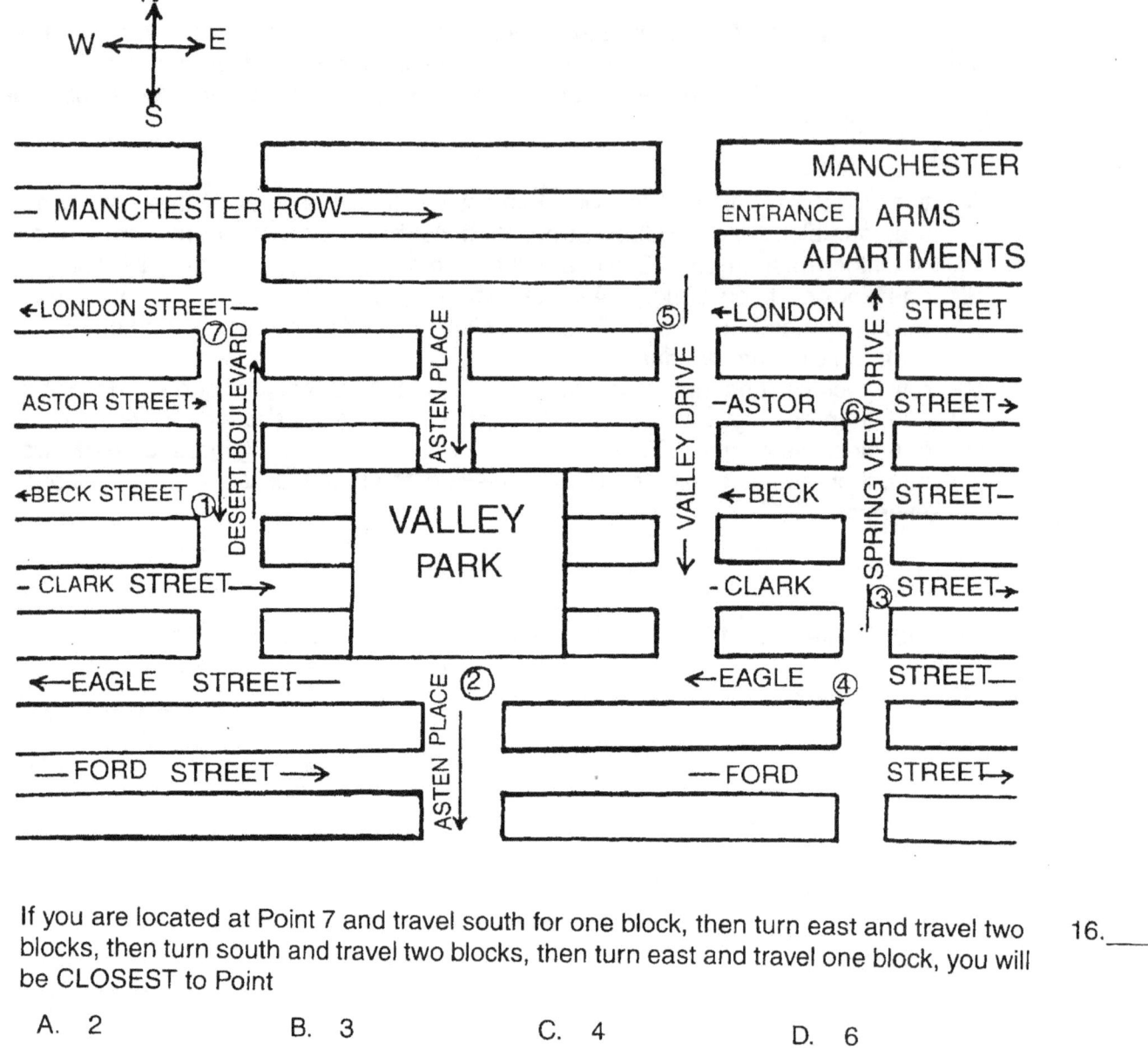

16. If you are located at Point 7 and travel south for one block, then turn east and travel two blocks, then turn south and travel two blocks, then turn east and travel one block, you will be CLOSEST to Point

    A. 2   B. 3   C. 4   D. 6

17. If you are located at Point 3 and travel north for one block, and then turn west and travel one block, and then turn south and travel two blocks, and then turn west and travel one block, you will be CLOSEST to Point

    A. 1   B. 2   C. 4   D. 6

18. You are located at Astor Street and Spring View Drive. You receive a call of a crime in progress at the intersection of Beck Street and Desert Boulevard.
    Which one of the following is the MOST direct route for you to take in your patrol car, making sure to obey all traffic regulations?
    Travel

    A. one block north on Spring View Drive, then three blocks west on London Street, then two blocks south on Desert Boulevard
    B. three blocks west on Astor Street, then one block south on Desert Boulevard

C. one block south on Spring View Drive, then three blocks west on Beck Street
D. three blocks south on Spring View Drive, then three blocks west on Eagle Street, then two blocks north on Desert Boulevard

19. You are located on Clark Street and Desert Boulevard and must respond to a disturbance at Clark Street and Spring View Drive.
Which one of the following is the MOST direct route for you to take in your patrol car, making sure to obey all traffic regulations?
Travel

   A. two blocks north on Desert Boulevard, then three blocks east on Astor Street, then two blocks south on Spring View Drive
   B. one block south on Desert Boulevard, then three blocks east on Eagle Street, then one block north on Spring View Drive
   C. two blocks north on Desert Boulevard, then two blocks east on Astor Street, then three blocks south on Valley Drive, then one block east on Eagle Street, then one block north on Spring View Drive
   D. two blocks north on Desert Boulevard, then two blocks east on Astor Street, then two blocks south on Valley Drive, then one block east on Clark Street

20. You are located at Valley Drive and Beck Street and receive a call to respond to the corner of Asten Place and Astor Street.
Which one of the following is the MOST direct route for you to take in your patrol car, making sure to obey all traffic regulations?
Travel _____ on Astor Street.

   A. one block north on Valley Drive, then one block west
   B. two blocks south on Valley Drive, then one block east on Eagle Street, then three blocks north on Spring View Drive, then two blocks west
   C. two blocks south on Valley Drive, then two blocks west on Eagle Street, then three blocks north on Desert Boulevard, then one block east
   D. one block south on Valley Drive, then one block east on Clark Street, then two blocks north on Spring View Drive, then two blocks west

KEY (CORRECT ANSWERS)

1.	C	11.	B
2.	A	12.	A
3.	A	13.	A
4.	D	14.	C
5.	C	15.	D
6.	B	16.	B
7.	C	17.	B
8.	B	18.	A
9.	A	19.	D
10.	A	20.	C

READING COMPREHENSION
UNDERSTANDING AND INTERPRETING WRITTEN MATERIAL
EXAMINATION SECTION
TEST 1

DIRECTIONS: Each question or incomplete statement is followed by several suggested answers or completions. Select the one that BEST answers the question or completes the statement. *PRINT THE LETTER OF THE CORRECT ANSWER IN THE SPACE AT THE RIGHT.*

Questions 1-3.

DIRECTIONS: Questions 1 through 3 are to be answered SOLELY on the basis of the following passage.

When police officers search for a stolen car, they first check for the color of the car, then for make, model, year, body damage, and finally license number. The first five can be detected from almost any angle, while the recognition of the license number is often not immediately apparent. The serial number and motor number, though less likely to be changed than the easily substituted license number, cannot be observed in initial detection of the stolen car.

1. According to the above passage, the one of the following features which is LEAST readily observed in checking for a stolen car in moving traffic is
   A. license number B. serial number C. model
   D. make   E. color

   1.____

2. The feature of a car that cannot be determined from most angles of observation is the
   A. make   B. model   C. year
   D. license number E. color

   2.____

3. Of the following, the feature of a stolen car that is MOST likely to be altered by a car thief shortly after the car is stolen is the
   A. license number B. motor number   C. color
   D. model   E. minor body damage

   3.____

Questions 4-5.

DIRECTIONS: Questions 4 and 5 are to be answered SOLELY on the basis of the following passage.

The racketeer is primarily concerned with business affairs, legitimate or otherwise, and preferably those which are close to the margin of legitimacy. He gets his best opportunities from business organizations which meet the need of large sections of the public for goods or services which are defined as illegitimate by the same public, such as prostitution, gambling, illicit drugs or liquor. In contrast to the thief, the racketeer and the establishments he controls deliver goods and services for money received.

4. From the above passage, it can be deduced that suppression of racketeers is difficult because
   A. victims of racketeers are not guilty of violating the law
   B. racketeers are generally engaged in fully legitimate enterprises
   C. many people want services which are not obtainable through legitimate sources
   D. the racketeers are well organized
   E. laws prohibiting gambling and prostitution are unenforceable

4._____

5. According to the above passage, racketeering, unlike theft, involves
   A. objects of value
   B. payment for goods received
   C. organized gangs
   D. public approval
   E. unlawful activities

5._____

Questions 6-8.

DIRECTIONS: Questions 6 through 8 are to be answered SOLELY on the basis of the following passage.

A number of crimes, such as robbery, assault, rape, certain forms of theft and burglary, are high visibility crimes in that it is apparent to all concerned that they are criminal acts prior to or at the time they are committed. In contrast to these, check forgeries, especially those committed by first offenders, have low visibility. There is little in the criminal act or in the interaction between the check passer and the person cashing the check to identify it as a crime. Closely related to this special quality of the forgery crime is the fact that, while it is formally defined and treated as a felonious or infamous crime, it is formally held by the legally untrained public to be a relatively harmless form of crime.

6. According to the above passage, crimes of *high visibility*
   A. are immediately recognized as crimes by the victim
   B. take place in public view
   C. always involve violence or the threat of violence
   D. usually are committed after dark
   E. can be observed from a distance

6._____

7. According to the above passage,
   A. the public regards check forgery as a minor crime
   B. the law regards check forgery as a minor crime
   C. the law distinguishes between check forgery and other forgery
   D. it is easier to spot inexperienced check forgers than other criminals
   E. it is more difficult to identify check forgers than other criminals

7._____

8. As used in the above passage, an *infamous* crime is
   A. a crime attracting great attention from the public
   B. more serious than a felony
   C. less serious than a felony
   D. more or less than a felony depending upon the surrounding circumstances
   E. the same as a felony

8._____

3 (#1)

Questions 9-11.

DIRECTIONS: Questions 9 through 11 are to be answered SOLELY on the basis of the following passage.

Criminal science is largely the science of identification. Progress in this field has been marked and sometimes very spectacular because new techniques, instruments, and facts flow continuously from the scientists. But the crime laboratories are undermanned, trade secrets still prevail, and inaccurate conclusions are often the results. However, modern gadgets cannot substitute for the skilled intelligent investigator; he must be their master.

9. According to the above passage, criminal science
   A. excludes the field of investigation
   B. is primarily interested in establishing identity
   C. is based on the equipment used in crime laboratories
   D. uses techniques different from those used in other sciences
   E. is essentially secret in nature

10. Advances in criminal science have been, according to the above passage,
    A. extremely limited
    B. slow but steady
    C. unusually reliable
    D. outstanding
    E. infrequently worthwhile

11. A problem that has NOT been overcome completely in crime work is, according to the above passage,
    A. unskilled investigators
    B. the expense of new equipment and techniques
    C. an insufficient number of personnel in crime laboratories
    D. inaccurate equipment used in laboratories
    E. conclusions of the public about the value of this field

Questions 12-14.

DIRECTIONS: Questions 12 through 14 are to be answered SOLELY on the basis of the following passage.

The New York City Police Department will accept for investigation no report of a person missing from his residence, if such residence is located outside of New York City. The person reporting same will be advised to report such fact to the police department of the locality where the missing person lives, which will, if necessary, communicate officially with the New York City Police Department. However, a report will be accepted of a person who is missing from a temporary residence in New York City, but the person making the report will be instructed to make a report also to the police department of the locality where the missing person lives.

12. According to the above passage, a report to the New York City Police Department of a missing person whose permanent residence is outside of New York City will
    A. always be investigated provided that a report is also made to his local police authorities

B. never be investigated unless requested officially by his local police authorities
C. be investigated in cases of temporary New York City residence, but a report should always be made to his local police authorities
D. be investigated if the person making the report is a New York City resident
E. always be investigated and a report will be made to the local police authorities by the New York City Police Department

13. Of the following, the MOST likely reason for the procedure described in the above passage is that
    A. non-residents are not entitled to free police service from New York City
    B. local police authorities would resent interference in their jurisdiction
    C. local police authorities sometimes try to unload their problems on the New York City Police
    D. local police authorities may be better able to conduct an investigation
    E. few persons are erroneously reported as missing

14. Mr. Smith, who lives in Jersey City, and Mr. Jones, who lives in Newark, arrange to meet in New York City, but Mr. Jones doesn't keep the appointment. Mr. Smith telephones Mr. Jones several times the next day and gets no answer. Mr. Smith believes that something has happened to Mr. Jones. According to the above passage, Mr. Smith should apply to the police authorities of
    A. Jersey City
    B. Newark
    C. Newark and New York City
    D. Jersey City and New York City
    E. Newark, Jersey City, and New York City

Questions 15-17.

DIRECTIONS: Questions 15 through 17 are to be answered SOLELY on the basis of the following passage.

Some early psychologists believed that the basic characteristic of the criminal type was inferiority of intelligence, if not outright feeblemindedness. They were misled by the fact that they had measurements for all kinds of criminals, but, until World War I gave them a draft army sample, they had no information on a comparable group of non-criminal adults. As soon as acceptable measurements could be taken of criminals and a comparable group of non-criminals, concern with feeblemindedness or with low intelligence as a type took on less and less significance in research in criminology.

15. According to the above passage, some early psychologists were in error because they didn't
    A. distinguish among the various types of criminals
    B. devise a suitable method of measuring intelligence
    C. measure the intelligence of non-criminals as a basis for comparison

D. distinguish between feeblemindedness and inferiority of intelligence
E. clearly define the term *intelligence*

16. The above passage implies that studies of the intelligence of criminals and non-criminals
    A. are useless because it is impossible to obtain comparable groups
    B. are not meaningful because only the less intelligent criminals are detected
    C. indicate that criminals are more intelligent than non-criminals
    D. indicate that criminals are less intelligent than non-criminals
    E. do not indicate that there are any differences between the two groups

16._____

17. According to the above passage, studies of the World War I draft gave psychologists vital information concerning
    A. adaptability to army life of criminals and non-criminals
    B. criminal tendencies among draftees
    C. the intelligence scores of large numbers of men
    D. differences between intelligence scores of draftees and volunteers
    E. the behavior of men under abnormal conditions

17._____

Questions 18-20.

DIRECTIONS: Questions 18 through 20 are to be answered SOLELY on the basis of the following passage.

The use of a roadblock is simply an adaptation to police practices of the military concept of encirclement. Successful operation of a roadblock plan depends almost entirely on the amount of advance study and planning given to such operations. A thorough and detailed examination of the roads and terrain under the jurisdiction of a given policy agency should be made with the locations of the roadblocks pinpointed in advance. The first principle to be borne in mind in the location of each roadblock is the time element. Its location must be at a point beyond which the fugitive could not have possibly traveled in the time elapsed from the commission of the crime to the arrival of the officers at the roadblock.

18. According to the above passage,
    A. military operations have made extensive use of roadblocks
    B. the military concept of encirclement is an adaptation of police use of roadblocks
    C. the technique of encirclement has been widely used by military forces
    D. a roadblock is generally more effective than encirclement
    E. police use of roadblocks is based on the idea of military encirclement

18._____

19. According to the above passage,
    A. the factor of time is the sole consideration in the location of a roadblock
    B. the maximum speed possible in the method of escape is of major importance in roadblock location
    C. the time of arrival of officers at the site of a proposed roadblock is of little importance

19._____

D. if the method of escape is not known, it should be assumed that the escape is by automobile
E. a roadblock should be sited as close to the scene of the crime as the terrain will permit

20. According to the above passage, 20.____
    A. advance study and planning are of minor importance in the success of roadblock operations
    B. a thorough and detailed examination of all roads within a radius of fifty miles should precede the determination of a roadblock location
    C. consideration of terrain features are important in planning the location of roadblocks
    D. the pinpointing of roadblocks should be performed before any advance study is made
    E. a roadblock operation can seldom be successfully undertaken by a single police agency

KEY (CORRECT ANSWERS)

1.	B	11.	C
2.	D	12.	C
3.	A	13.	D
4.	C	14.	B
5.	B	15.	C
6.	A	16.	E
7.	A	17.	C
8.	E	18.	E
9.	B	19.	B
10.	D	20.	C

TEST 2

DIRECTIONS: Each question or incomplete statement is followed by several suggested answers or completions. Select the one that BEST answers the question or completes the statement. *PRINT THE LETTER OF THE CORRECT ANSWER IN THE SPACE AT THE RIGHT.*

Questions 1-3.

DIRECTIONS: Questions 1 through 3 are to be answered SOLELY on the basis of the following passage.

Modern police science may be said to have three phases. The first phase embraces the identification of living and dead persons. The second embraces the field work carried out by specially trained detectives at the scene of the crime. The third embraces methods used in the police laboratory to examine and analyze clues and traces discovered in the course of the investigation. While modern police science has had a striking influence on detective work and will surely further enhance its effectiveness, the time-honored methods and practical detective work will always be important. The time-honored methods, that is knowledge of methods used by criminals, patience, tact, industry, thoroughness, and imagination, will always be requisites for successful detective work.

1. According to the above passage, we may expect modern police science to   1.____
   A. help detective work more and more
   B. become more and more scientific
   C. depend less and less on the time-honored methods
   D. bring together the many different approaches to detective work
   E. play a less important role in detective work

2. According to the above passage, a knowledge of the procedures used by   2.____
   criminals is
   A. solely an element of the modern police science approach to detective work
   B. related to the identification of persons
   C. not related to detective field work
   D. related to methods used in the police laboratory
   E. an element of the traditional approach to detective work

3. Modern police science and practical detective work, according to the above   3.____
   passage,
   A. when used together can only lead to confusion
   B. are based distinctly different theories of detective work
   C. have had strikingly different influence on detective work
   D. should both be used for successful detective work
   E. lead usually to similar results

Questions 4-7.

DIRECTIONS: Questions 4 through 7 are to be answered SOLELY on the basis of the following passage.

A member of the force shall render reasonable aid to a sick or injured person. He shall summon an ambulance, if necessary, by telephoning the communications bureau of the borough, who shall notify the precinct concerned. If possible, he shall wait in full view of the arriving ambulance and take necessary action to direct the responding doctor or attendant to the patient, without delay. If the ambulance does not arrive in twenty minutes, he shall send in a second call. However, if the sick person is in his or her own home, a member of the force, before summoning an ambulance, will ascertain whether such person is willing to be taken to a hospital for treatment.

4. According to the above passage, if a patrolman wants to get an ambulance for a sick person, he should telephone
   A. the precinct concerned
   B. only if the sick person is in his home
   C. the nearest hospital
   D. only if the sick person is not in his home
   E. the borough communications bureau

5. According to the above passage, if a patrolman telephones for an ambulance and none arrives within twenty minutes, he should
   A. ask the injured person if he is willing to be taken to a hospital
   B. call the borough communications bureau
   C. call the precinct concerned
   D. attempt to give the injured person such assistance as he may need
   E. call the nearest hospital

6. A patrolman is called to help a woman who has fallen in her own home and has apparently broken her leg.
   According to the above passage, he should
   A. ask her if she wants to go to a hospital
   B. try to set her leg if it is necessary
   C. call for an ambulance at once
   D. attempt to get a doctor as quickly as possible
   E. not attempt to help the woman in any way before competent medical aid arrives

7. A man falls from a window into the backyard of an apartment house. Assume that you are a patrolman and that you are called to assist this man.
   According to the above passage, after you have called for an ambulance and comforted the injured man as much as you can, you should
   A. wait in front of the house for the ambulance
   B. ask the injured man if he wishes to go to the hospital for treatment
   C. remain with the injured man until the ambulance arrives
   D. send a bystander to direct the nearest doctor to the patient
   E. not ask the man to explain how the accident happened

Questions 8-10.

DIRECTIONS: Questions 8 through 10 are to be answered SOLELY on the basis of the following passage.

What is required is a program that will protect our citizens and their property from criminal and antisocial acts, will effectively restrain and reform juvenile delinquents, and will prevent the further development of antisocial behavior. Discipline and punishment of offenders must necessarily play an important part in any such program. Serious offenders cannot be mollycoddled merely because they are under twenty-one. Restraint and punishment necessarily follow serious antisocial acts. But punishment, if it is to be effective, must be a planned part of a more comprehensive program of treating delinquency.

8. The one of the following goals NOT included among those listed above is to 8.____
   A. stop young people from defacing public property
   B. keep homes from being broken into
   C. develop an intra-city boys' baseball league
   D. change juvenile delinquents into useful citizens
   E. prevent young people from developing antisocial behavior patterns

9. According to the above passage, punishment is 9.____
   A. not satisfactory in any program dealing with juvenile delinquents
   B. the most effective means by which young vandals and hooligans can be reformed
   C. not used sufficiently when dealing with serious offenders who are under twenty-one
   D. of value in reducing juvenile delinquency only if it is part of a complete program
   E. most effective when it does not relate to specific antisocial acts

10. With respect to serious offenders who are under twenty-one, the above passage suggests that they 10.____
    A. be mollycoddled
    B. be dealt with as part of a comprehensive program to punish mature criminals
    C. should be punished
    D. be prevented, by brute force if necessary, from performing antisocial acts
    E. be treated as delinquent children who require more love than punishment

Questions 11-14.

DIRECTIONS: Questions 11 through 14 are to be answered SOLELY on the basis of the following passage.

In all cases of homicide, members of the Police Department who investigate will make every effort to obtain statements from dying persons. Such statements are of the greatest importance to the District Attorney. In many cases, there may be a failure to solve the crime if they are not taken. The principle element to be considered in taking the declaration of a dying person is his mental attitude. In order to be admissible in evidence, the person must have no hope of recovery. The patient will be fully interrogated on that point before a statement is taken.

11. In cases of homicide, according to the above passage, members of the police force will
    A. try to change the mental attitude of the dying person
    B. attempt to obtain a statement from the dying person
    C. not give the information they obtain directly to the District Attorney
    D. be careful not to injure the dying person unnecessarily
    E. prevent unauthorized persons from taking dying declarations

11.____

12. The mental attitude of the person making the dying statement is of great importance because it can determine, according to the above passage, whether the
    A. victim should be interrogated in the presence of witnesses
    B. victim will be willing to make a statement of any kind
    C. victim has been forced to make the statement
    D. statement will tell the District Attorney who committed the crime
    E. statement can be used as evidence

12.____

13. District Attorneys find that statements of a dying person are important, according to the above passage, because
    A. it may be that the victim will recover and refuse to testify
    B. they are important elements in determining the mental attitude of the victim
    C. they present a point of view
    D. it may be impossible to punish the criminal without such a statement
    E. dead men tell no tales

13.____

14. A well-known gangster is found dying from a bullet wound. The patrolman first on the scene, in the presence of witnesses, tells the man that he is going to die and asks, *Who shot you?* The gangster says, *Jones shot me, but he hasn't killed me. I'll live to get him.* He then falls back dead.
    According to the above passage, this statement is
    A. *admissible* in evidence; the man was obviously speaking the truth
    B. *not admissible* in evidence; the man obviously did not believe that he was dying
    C. *admissible* in evidence; there were witnesses to the statement
    D. *not admissible* in evidence; the victim did not sign any statement and the evidence is merely hearsay
    E. *admissible* in evidence; there was no time to interrogate the victim

14.____

Questions 15-17.

DIRECTIONS: Questions 15 through 17 are to be answered SOLELY on the basis of the following passage.

The factors contributing to crime and delinquency are varied and complex. The home and its immediate environment have been found to be crucial in determining the behavior patterns of the individual, and criminality can frequently be traced to faulty family relationships and a bad neighborhood. But in the search for a clearer understanding of the underlying causes of delinquent and criminal behavior, the total environment must be taken into consideration.

15. According to the above passage, family relationships 15.____
    A. tend to become faulty in bad neighborhoods
    B. are important in determining the actions of honest people as well as criminals
    C. are the only important element in the understanding of causes of delinquency
    D. are determined by the total environment
    E. of criminals are understandable only in terms of the behavior patterns of the individuals concerned

16. According to the above passage, the causes of crime and delinquency are 16.____
    A. not simple   B. not meaningless
    C. meaningless   D. simple
    E. always understandable

17. According to the above passage, faulty family relationships frequently are 17.____
    A. responsible for varied and complex results
    B. caused by differences
    C. caused when one or both parents have a criminal behavior pattern
    D. independent of the total environment
    E. the cause of criminal acts

Questions 18-20.

DIRECTIONS: Questions 18 through 20 are to be answered SOLELY on the basis of the following passage.

A change in the specific problems which confront the police and in the methods for dealing with them has taken place in the last few decades. The automobile is a two-way symbol of this change in policing. It menaces every city with a complicated traffic problem and has speeded up the process of committing a crime and making a getaway, but at the same time has increased the effectiveness of police operations. However, the major concern of police departments continues to be the antisocial or criminal actions and behavior of human beings.

18. On the basis of the above passage, it can be stated that for the most part in 18.____
    the past few decades, the specific problems of a police force
    A. have changed but the general problems have not
    B. as well as the general problems have changed
    C. have remained the same but the general problems have changed
    D. as well as the general problems have remained the same
    E. have caused changes in the general problems

19. According to the above passage, advances in science and industry have, in general, made the police
    A. operations less effective from the overall point of view
    B. operations more effective from the overall point of view
    C. abandon older methods of solving police problems
    D. concern themselves more with the antisocial acts of human beings
    E. concern themselves less with the antisocial acts of human beings

20. The automobile is a *two-way symbol*, according to the above passage, because its use
    A. has speeded up getting to, and away from, the scene of a crime
    B. both helps and hurts police operations
    C. introduces a new antisocial act—traffic violation—and does away with criminals like horse thieves
    D. both increases and decreases speed by introducing traffic problems
    E. helps people get to the city but prevents them from moving once they are there

KEY (CORRECT ANSWERS)

1.	A		11.	B
2.	E		12.	E
3.	D		13.	D
4.	E		14.	B
5.	B		15.	B
6.	A		16.	A
7.	A		17.	E
8.	C		18.	A
9.	D		19.	B
10.	C		20.	B

REPORT WRITING

EXAMINATION SECTION

TEST 1

DIRECTIONS: Each question or incomplete statement is followed by several suggested answers or completions. Select the one that BEST answers the question or completes the statement. *PRINT THE LETTER OF THE CORRECT ANSWER IN THE SPACE AT THE RIGHT.*

Questions 1-5.

DIRECTIONS: Questions 1 through 5 are to be answered SOLELY on the basis of the following report.

REPORT OF DEFECTIVE EQUIPMENT

DEPARTMENT: *Social Services*   REPORT NO. 3026
DIVISION: *Personnel*   DATE OF REPORT: *5/27*
ROOM: 120B

DEFECTIVE EQUIPMENT: *Six office telephones with pick-up and hold buttons*

DESCRIPTION OF DEFECT: *Marjorie Black, a Clerk, called on 5/22 to report that the button lights for the four lines on all six telephones in her office were not functioning and it was, therefore, impossible to know which lines were in use. On 5/26, Howard Perl, Admin. Asst., called in regard to the same telephones. He was annoyed because no repairs had been made and stated that all the employees in his unit were being inconvenienced. He requested prompt repair service.*

Ruth Gomez
SIGNATURE OF REPORTING EMPLOYEE
Sr. Telephone Operator
TITLE

JUDITH O'LAUGHLIN
SIGNATURE OF SUPERVISOR

TO BE COMPLETED AFTER SERVICING
DATE: 5/28
APPROVED: *Judy O'Laughlin*

---

1. The person who made a written report about the improper functioning of telephones in the Personnel division is
    A. Marjorie Black
    B. Ruth Gomez
    C. Howard Perl
    D. Judith O'Laughlin

1.____

2. How many days elapsed between the original request for telephone repair service and the completion of service?
   A. 2   B. 4   C. 5   D. 6

3. Of the following, the only information NOT given in the report is
   A. number of employees affected by the defective service
   B. number of the report
   C. number of telephones with a button defect
   D. telephone numbers of the defective phones

4. The one of the following items of information which would have been LEAST helpful to the repairman who was assigned this repair job is that
   A. the defect involved pick-up buttons for 4 serviced lines
   B. the location is Room 120B in the Department of Social Services
   C. Marjorie Black initially reported the defective equipment
   D. six telephone units need to be repaired

5. Which of the following statements is CORRECT concerning the people mentioned in the report?
   A. Ruth Gomez has a higher titled than Judith O'Laughlin
   B. Judith O'Laughlin's signature appears twice on this form
   C. Howard Perl reported on May 25 that the telephones needed adjusting
   D. Marjorie Black reported that she was disturbed that no repairs had been made

Questions 6-10.

DIRECTIONS: Questions 6 through 10 are based on the UNUSUAL OCCURRENCE REPORT given below. Five phrases in the report have been removed and are listed below the report as 1. through 5. in each of the five places where phrases of the report have been left out, the number of a question has been inserted. For each question, select the number of the missing phrase which would make the report read correctly.

UNUSUAL OCCURRENCE REPORT

POST _____
TOUR _____
DATE _____

Location of Occurrence:_____
REMARKS: While making rounds this morning, I thought that I heard some strange sounds coming from Storeroom #55. Upon investigation, I saw that 6 and that the door to the storeroom was slightly opened. At 2:45 A.M. I 7.

Suddenly two men jumped out from 8, dropped the tools which they were holding, and made a dash for the door. I ordered them to stop, but they just kept running.

3 (#1)

I was able to get a good look at both of them. One man was wearing a green jacket and had a full beard, and the other was short and had blond hair. Immediately, I called the police; and about two minutes later, I notified 9. I 10 the police arrived, and I gave them the complete details of the incident.

                                          Security Officer Donald Rimson   23807
                                                    Signature   Pass No.

1. the special inspection control desk
2. behind some crates
3. the lock had been tampered with
4. remained at the storeroom unit
5. entered the storeroom and began to look around

6. A. 1   B. 3   C. 4   D. 5   6.____

7. A. 2   B. 3   C. 4   D. 5   7.____

8. A. 1   B. 2   C. 3   D. 4   8.____

9. A. 1   B. 2   C. 3   D. 4   9.____

10. A. 2   B. 3   C. 4   D. 5   10.____

Questions 11-13.

DIRECTIONS: Below is a report consisting of 15 numbered sentences, some of which are not consistent with the principles of good report writing. Questions 11 through 13 are to be answered SOLELY on the basis of the information contained in the report and your knowledge of investigative principles and practices.

To: Tom Smith, Administrative Investigator
From: John Jones, Supervising Investigator

1. On January 7, I received a call from Mrs. H. Harris of 684 Sunset Street, Brooklyn.
2. Mr. Harris informed me that she wanted to report an instance of fraud relating to public assistance payments being received by her neighbor, Mrs. I Wallace.
3. I advised her that such a subject would best be discussed in person.
4. I then arranged a field visitation for January 10 at Mrs. Harris' apartment, 684 Sunset Street, Brooklyn.
5. On January 10, I discussed the basis for Mrs. Harris' charge against Mrs. Wallace at the former's apartment.
6. She stated that her neighbor is receiving Aid to Dependent Children payments for seven children, but that only three of her children are still living with her.
7. In addition, Mrs. Harris also claimed that her husband, whom she reported to the authorities as missing, usually sees her several times a week.
8. After further questioning, Mrs. Harris admitted to me that she had been quite friendly with Mrs. Wallace until they recently argued about trash left in their adjoining hall corridor.

9. However, she firmly stated that her allegations against Mrs. Wallace were valid and that she feared repercussions for her actions.
10. At the completion of the interview, I assured Mrs. Harris of the confidentiality of her statements and that an attempt would be made to verify her allegations.
11. As I was leaving Mrs. Harris' apartment, I noticed a man, aged approximately 45, walking out of Mrs. Wallace's apartment.
12. I followed him until he entered an old green Oldsmobile and sped away.
13. On January 3, I returned to 684 Sunset Court, having determined that Mrs. Wallace is receiving assistance as indicated by Mrs. Harris.
14. However, upon presentation of official identification Mrs. Wallace refused to admit me to her apartment or grant an interview.
15. I am therefore referring this matter to you for further instructions.

John Jones
Supervising Investigator

11. The one of the following statements that clearly lacks vital information is Statement 11.____
    A. 8   B. 10   C. 12   D. 14

12. Which of the following sentences from the report is ambiguous? 12.____
    A. 2   B. 3   C. 7   D. 10

13. Which of the following sentences contains information contradicting other data in the above report? Sentence 13.____
    A. 3   B. 8   C. 10   D. 13

Questions 14-16.

DIRECTIONS: Questions 14 through 16 are to be answered on the basis of the following report.

To: Ralph King
    Senior Menagerie Keeper

Date: April 3
Subject:

From: William Rattner
       Menagerie Keeper

This memorandum is to inform you of the disappearance of the boa constrictor from the Reptile Collection in the Main Building.

This morning upon entering the room, I realized that the snake was missing. After having asked around, I am of the opinion that the boa constrictor has been stolen. Since there are no signs of forced entry, it seems likely that whoever removed the snake from the premises entered the room through a window which had been left unlocked the previous night. I, therefore, suggest that all zoo personnel be more concerned with proper security measures in the future so that something like this does not happen again.

14. Which one of the following pieces of information has been OMITTED from the report by the Menagerie Keeper? 14.____
    A. Action taken by him after his discovery that the boa constrictor was missing
    B. The date that the disappearance of the boa constrictor was noted
    C. The time that the disappearance of the boa constrictor was noted
    D. The building in which the boa constrictor was kept

15. Based upon information contained in the above paragraph, which of the following statements would be BEST as the subject of this report? 15.____
    A. Request for more effective security measures in the oo
    B. Vandalism in the zoo
    C. Disappearance of boa constrictor
    D. Request for replacement of boa constrictor

16. According to the above report, which of the following statements CANNOT be considered factual? 16.____
    A. The boa constrictor was being kept in the Main Building
    B. The boa constrictor is missing
    C. All zoo personnel are careless about security measures
    D. There are no signs of forced entry

Questions 17-19.

DIRECTIONS: Questions 17 through 19 are to be answered on the basis of the Accident Report below. Read this report carefully before answering the questions. Select your answers ONLY on the basis of this report.

ACCIDENT REPORT

February 14

On February 14 at 3:45 P.M., Mr. Warren, while on the top of a stairway at the 34th Street Station, realized the *D* train was in the station loading passengers. In this haste to catch the train, he forcefully ran down the stairs, pushing aside three other people also going down the stairs. Mr. Parker, one of the three people, lost his footing and fell to the bottom of the stairs. Working on the platform, I saw Mr. Parker lose his footing as a result of Mr. Warren's actions, and I immediately went to his aid. Assistant Station Supervisor Brown was attracted to the incident after a crowd had gathered. After 15 minutes, the injured man, Mr. Parker, got up and boarded a train that was in the station and, therefore, he was not hurt seriously.

R. Sands #3214
Conductor

17. Since accident reports should only contain facts, which of the following should NOT be put into the accident report?
    A. The incident took place at the 34th Street Station.
    B. Mr. Parker was not hurt seriously.
    C. The date that the report was written
    D. Mr. Sands went to the aid of the injured an

18. The title of the person submitting the report was 18.____
    A. Porter
    B. Assistant Station Supervisor
    C. Conductor
    D. Passenger

19. The TOTAL number of different persons mentioned in this report is 19.____
    A. seven B. six C. five D. four

Questions 20-24.

DIRECTIONS: Questions 20 through 24 are to be answered SOLELY on the basis of the following report which is similar to those used in departments for reporting accidents,

REPORT OF ACCIDENT

Date of Accident 3/21   Tim: 3:43 P.M.   Date of Report: 3/24

Department Vehicle
Operator's Name: James Doe
Title: Motor Vehicle Operator
Vehicle Code No. 22-187
License Plate No.: 3N-1234

Damage to Vehicle: Right rear fender ripped, hubcap dented, rear bumper twisted
Place of Accident: 8th Avenue & 48th Street

Vehicle No. 2
Operator's Name: Richard Roe
Operator's Address: 841 W. 68th St.
Owner' Name: Jane Roe
Owner's Address: 2792 Beal Ave.
License Plate No. 8Y-6789

Damage to Vehicle: Grill, radiator, right side of front bumper, right-front fender and headlight crushed.

Description of Accident: I was driving east on 48th Street with the green light. I was almost across 8th Avenue when Ford panel truck started forth and crashed into my rear right fender. Denver of Ford used abusive language and accused me of rolling into his truck.

Persons Injured

Name Richard Roe   Address 841 W. 68TH Street
Name _____   Address _____
Name _____   Address _____

20. Witnesses

Name Richard Roe   Address 841 W. 68th Street
Name John Brown   Address 226 South Avenue
Name Mary Green   Address 42 East Street

Report Prepared By James Doe
Title MVO Badge No. 11346

7 (#1)

20. According to the above description of the accident, the diagram that would BEST show how and where the vehicles crashed is

A.

B.

C.

D.

21. Of the following words used in the report, the one spelled INCORRECTLY is
 A. abussive B. accused C. radiator D. twisted

22. The city vehicle involved in this accident can BEST be identified
 A. as a panel truck
 B. the Department vehicle
 C. by the Badge Number of the operator
 D. by the Vehicle Code Number

23. According to the information in the report, the right-of-way belonged to
 A. neither vehicle   B. the Department vehicle
 C. the vehicle that took it   D. Vehicle No. 2

24. An entry on the report that seems to be INCORRECT is the
 A. first witness   B. second witness
 C. third witness   D. owner's name

25. Assume that the following passage is taken from a report which you, a deputy chief, receive from a battalion chief under your command. The report relates to a fire for which the department received public criticism because of delay in response and extension of fire to neighboring buildings. *Alarm from box ____ was received at 5:13 P.M. on Friday, October 2. All first alarm companies departed from quarters expeditiously but progress along the vehicle-glutted arterial thoroughfare was agonizingly slow. By dint of*

extraordinary effort and by virtue of great skill in maneuvering through impassable traffic, Engine Co. _____ arrived at the scene at 5:21 P.M. The sight which greeted them was a virtual Dante's INFERNO, of holocaust proportions. The hub of the conflagration was the penultimate structure of a row of houses, with extension impending to contiguous edifices.
The MAIN fault with the above report is that it
- A. contains spelling and punctuation errors
- B. contains unnecessary details
- C. uses words not in accordance with dictionary definitions
- D. uses inappropriate language and style.

KEY (CORRECT ANSWERS)

1.	B		11.	C
2.	D		12.	C
3.	A		13.	D
4.	C		14.	C
5.	B		15.	C
6.	B		16.	C
7.	D		17.	B
8.	B		18.	C
9.	A		19.	B
10.	C		20.	A

21.	A
22.	D
23.	B
24.	A
25.	D

TEST 2

DIRECTIONS: Each question or incomplete statement is followed by several suggested answers or completions. Select the one that BEST answers the question or completes the statement. *PRINT THE LETTER OF THE CORRECT ANSWER IN THE SPACE AT THE RIGHT.*

Questions 1-4.

DIRECTIONS: Questions 1 through 4 are to be answered on the basis of the information in the report below.

On February 15, Mr. Smith and Mr. Brown were injured in an accident occurring in the shop at 10 Long Road. No one was in the area of the accident other than Mr. Smith and Mr. Brown. Both of these employees described the following circumstances.

1. Mr. Brown saw the largest tool on the wall begin to fall from where it was hanging and run up to push Mr. Smith out of the way and to prevent the tool from falling, if possible.
2. Mr. Smith was standing near the wall under some tools which were hanging on nails in the wall.
3. Mr. Brown was standing a few steps from the wall.
4. Mr. Brown stepped toward Mr. Smith, who was on the floor and away from the falling tool. He tripped and fell over a piece of equipment on the floor.
5. Mr. Brown pushed Mr. Smith, who slipped on some grease on the floor and fell to the side, out of the way of the falling tool.
6. Mr. Brown tried to avoid Mr. Smith as he fell. In so doing, he fell against some pipes which were leaning against the wall. The pipes fell on both Mr. Brown and Mr. Smith.

Mr. Smith and Mr. Brown were both badly bruised and shaken. They were sent to the General Hospital to determine if any bones were broken. The office was later notified that neither employee was seriously hurt.

Since the accident, matters relating to safety and accident prevention around the shop have occupied the staff. There have been a number of complaints about the location of tools and equipment. Several employees are reluctant to work in the shop unless conditions are improved. Please advise as to the best way to handle this situation.

1. The one of the following which it is MOST important to add to the above memorandum is
   A. a signature line
   B. a transmittal note
   C. the date of the memo
   D. the initials of the typist

2. The MOST logical order in which to list the circumstances relative to the accident is
   A. as shown (1, 2, 3, 4, 5, 6)
   B. 2, 3, 1, 5, 4, 6
   C. 1, 5, 4, 6, 3, 2
   D. 3, 2, 4, 6, 1, 5

3. The one of the following which does NOT properly belong with the rest of the memorandum is
   A. the first section of paragraph 1
   B. the list of circumstances
   C. paragraph 2
   D. paragraph 3

3._____

4. According to the information in the memorandum, the BEST description of the subject is:
   A. Effect of accident on work output of the division
   B. Description of accident involving Mr. Smith and Mr. Brown
   C. Recommendations on how to avoid future accidents
   D. Safety and accident control in the shop

4._____

Questions 5-10.

DIRECTIONS: A ferry terminal supervisor is asked to write a report on the incident described in the following passage. Questions 5 through 10 are to be answered on the basis of the incident and the supervisor's report. Your answers should be based on the assumption that everything described in the passage is true.

On July 27, a rainy, foggy day, Joseph Jones and Steven Smith were in the Whitehall Ferry Terminal at about 9:50 A.M. waiting for the 10:00 A.M. ferry to Staten Island. Smith, seated with his legs stretched out in the aisle, was reading the sports page of the DAILY NEWS. Jones was walking by, drinking ginger ale from a cup. Neither man paid any attention to the other until Jones tripped over Smith's foot, fell to the floor, and dropped his drink. Smith looked at Jones as he lay on the floor and burst out laughing. Jones, infuriated, got up and punched Smith in the jaw. The force of the blow drove Smith's head back against the bench on which he was sitting. Smith did not fight back; he appeared to be dazed. Bystanders called a terminal worker, who assisted in making Smith as comfortable as possible.

One of the other people in the terminal for the ferry was a nurse, who examined Smith and told the ferry terminal supervisor that Smith probably had a concussion. An ambulance was called to take Smith to the hospital. A policeman arrived on the scene.

Jones' injury consisted of a sprained ankle and some bruises, but he refused medical attention. Jones explained to the supervisor what had happened. Jones truly regretted what he had done and went to the local police station with the policeman.

5. Of the following facts about the above incident, which one would be MOST important to include in the ferry terminal supervisor's report?
   A. The time the next boat was due to arrive
   B. Jones was carrying a cup of ginger ale
   C. Smith was sitting with his legs stretched out in the aisle
   D. Why Smith and Jones were in the terminal

5._____

6. The MAIN purpose of writing a report of the above incident is to
   A. make recommendations for preventing fights in the terminal
   B. state the important facts of the incident
   C. blame Jones for not looking where he was going
   D. provide evidence that Smith was not at fault

6._____

7. An adequate report of the above incident MUST give the names of the participants, the names of witnesses, and the
   A. date, the place, the time, and the events that took place
   B. date, the events that took place, the time, and the names of the terminal personnel on duty that day
   C. place, the names of the terminal personnel on duty that day, the weather conditions, and the events which took place
   D. names of the passengers in the terminal, the time, the place, and the events which took place

8. The supervisor asked for individuals who had witnessed the entire incident to give their account of what they had seen. Thomas White, a twelve-year-old boy said that Jones fell, got up, turned, and then hit Smith.
Thomas White's description of the incident is
   A. *adequate*; it is truthful, straight-forward, and includes necessary details
   B. *adequate;* it shows that the incident was not started on purpose
   C. *inadequate*; he is too young to understand the implications of his testimony
   D. *inadequate*; it omits certain pertinent facts about the incident

9. Another witness, Mary Collins, told the ferry terminal supervisor that when she heard Jones fall, she looked in that direction and saw Jones get up and hit Smith, who was laughing. She immediately ran to find a terminal worker to prevent further fighting. When she returned, she found Smith slumped on the bench.
Mrs. Collins' report is USEFUL because
   A. it proves that Smith antagonized Jones
   B. it indicates that Jones beat Smith repeatedly
   C. she witnessed that Jones hit Smith
   D. it shows that only one punch was thrown

10. Based on the description given above, which of the following would be the MOST accurate summary for the ferry terminal supervisor to put in his report?
    A. Jones fell and Smith laughed, which caused Jones to beat him until bystanders got a terminal worker to separate them.
    B. Smith was reading a newspaper when Jones fell. Then Jones hit Smith and dazed him. Smith was examined by a nurse who said that Smith had a serious concussion.
    C. Jones tripped accidentally over Smith's legs and fell. Smith laughed at Jones, who lost his temper and hit Smith, driving Smith's head against the back of a bench.
    D. Smith antagonized Jones first, by tripping him second, by laughing at him, and third by not fighting back. Smith was aided by a nurse and went to the hospital.

Questions 11-13.

DIRECTIONS: Questions 11 through 13 are to be answered SOLELY on the basis of the following report.

To: John Greene
    General Park Foreman

Date: May 5

From: Earl Jones
      Gardener

Subject:

On May 3rd, as I was finishing a job six feet from the boat-house, I observed that the hole which had been filled in last week was now not level with the ground around it. This seems to be a hazardous condition because it might cause pedestrians to fall into it. I, therefore, suggest that this job be redone as soon as possible.

11. This report should be considered poorly written MAINLY because
    A. it does not give enough information to take appropriate action
    B. too many different tenses are used
    C. it describes no actual personal injury to anyone
    D. there is no recommendation in the report to remedy the situation

12. It is noted that the subject of the report has been left out.
    Which of the following statements would be BEST as the subject of this report?
    A. Observation made by Earl Jones, Gardener
    B. Deteriorating condition of park grounds
    C. Report of dangerous condition near boathouse
    D. A dangerous walk through the park

13. In order for John Greene to take appropriate action, additional information should be added to the report giving the
    A. exact date the repair was made
    B. exact location of the hole
    C. exact time the observation was made
    D. names of the crew who previously filled in the hole

Questions 14-18.

DIRECTIONS: Questions 14 through 18 consist of sets of four sentences lettered A, B, C, and D. For each question, choose the sentence which is grammatically and stylistically MOST appropriate for use in a formal written report.

14. A. It is recommended, therefore, that the impasse panel hearings are to be convened on September 30.
    B. It is therefore recommended that the impasse panel hearings be convened on September 30.
    C. Therefore, it is recommended to convene the impasse panel hearings on September 30.
    D. It is recommended that the impasse panel hearings therefore should be convened on September 30.

15.
- A. Penalties have been assessed for violating the Taylor Law by several unions.
- B. When they violated provisions of the Taylor Law, several unions were later penalized.
- C. Several unions have been penalized for violating provisions of the Taylor Law.
- D. Several unions' violating provisions of the Taylor Law resulted in them being penalized.

16.
- A. The number of disputes settled through mediation has increased significantly over the past two years.
- B. The number of disputes settled through mediation are increasing significantly over two-year periods.
- C. Over the past two years, through mediation, the number of disputes settled increased significantly.
- D. There is a significant increase over the past two years of the number of disputes settled through mediation.

17.
- A. The union members will vote to determine if the contract is to be approved.
- B. It is not yet known whether the union members will ratify the proposed contract.
- C. When the union members vote, that will determine the new contract.
- D. Whether the union members will ratify the proposed contract, it is not yet known.

18.
- A. The parties agreed to an increase in fringe benefits in return for greater worker productivity.
- B. Greater productivity was agreed to be provided in return for increased fringe benefits.
- C. Productivity and fringe benefits are interrelated; the higher the former, the more the latter grows.
- D. The contract now provides that the amount of fringe benefits will depend upon the level of output by the workers.

19. Of the following excerpts, selected from letters, the one which is considered by modern letter writing experts to be the BEST is:
- A. Attached please find the application form to be filled out by you. Return the form to this office at the above address.
- B. Forward to this office your check accompanied by the application form enclosed with this letter.
- C. If you wish to apply, please complete and return the enclosed form with your check.
- D. In reply to your letter of December _____, enclosed herewith please find the application form you requested.

20. A city employee who writes a letter requesting information from a businessman should realize that, of the following, it is MOST important to
    A. end the letter with a polite closing
    B. make the letter short enough to fit on one page
    C. use a form, such as a questionnaire, to save the businessman's time
    D. use a courteous tone that will get the desired cooperation

Questions 21-22.

DIRECTIONS: Questions 21 and 22 consist of four sentences. Choose the one sentence in each set of four that would be BEST for a formal letter or report. Consider grammar and appropriate usage.

21. A. Most all the work he completed before he become ill.
    B. He completed most of the work before becoming ill.
    C. Prior to him becoming ill, his work was mostly completed.
    D. Before he became ill most of the work he had completed.

22. A. Being that the report lacked a clearly worded recommendation, it did not matter that it contained enough information.
    B. There was enough information in the report, although it, including the recommendation, were not clearly worded.
    C. Although the report contained enough information, it did not have a clearly worded recommendation.
    D. Though the report did not have a recommendation that was clearly worded, and the information therein contained was enough.

Questions 23-25.

DIRECTIONS: In Questions 23 through 25, choose the sentence which is BEST from the point of view of English usage suitable for a business letter or report.

23. A. Answering of veterans' inquiries, together with the receipt of fees, have been handled by the Bursar's Office since the new President came.
    B. Since the new President's arrival, the handling of all veteran's inquiries has been turned over to the Bursar's Office.
    C. In addition to the receipt of fees, the Bursar's Office has been handling veterans' inquiries since the new President came.
    D. The principle change in the work of the Bursar's Office since the new President came is that it now handles veterans' inquiries as well as the receipt of fees.

24. A. The current unrest about education undoubtedly stems in part from the fact that the people fear the basic purposes of the schools are being neglected or supplanted by spurious ones.
    B. The fears of people that the basic purposes of the schools are being neglected or supplanted by spurious ones contributes to the current unrest about education.

C. Undoubtedly some responsibility for the current unrest about education must be assigned to peoples' fears that the purpose and base of the school system is being neglected or supplanted.
D. From the fears of people that the basic purposes of the schools are being neglected or supplanted by spurious ones undoubtedly stem in part the current unrest about education.

25. A. The existence of administrative phenomena are clearly established, but their characteristics, relations and laws are obscure.
B. The obscurity of the characteristics, relations and laws of administrative phenomena do not preclude their existence.
C. Administrative phenomena clearly exists in spite of the obscurity of their characteristics, relations and laws.
D. The characteristics, relations and laws of administrative phenomena are obscure but the existence of the phenomena is clear.

25.____

KEY (CORRECT ANSWERS)

1.	C	11.	A
2.	B	12.	C
3.	D	13.	B
4.	B	14.	B
5.	C	15.	C
6.	B	16.	A
7.	A	17.	B
8.	D	18.	A
9.	C	19.	C
10.	C	20.	D

21. B
22. C
23. C
24. A
25. D

TEST 3

DIRECTIONS: Each question or incomplete statement is followed by several suggested answers or completions. Select the one that BEST answers the question or completes the statement. *PRINT THE LETTER OF THE CORRECT ANSWER IN THE SPACE AT THE RIGHT.*

1. Of the following, the BEST statement concerning the placement of *Conclusions and Recommendations* in a management report is:
   A. Recommendations should always be included in a report unless the report presents the results of an investigation.
   B. If a report presents conclusions, it must present recommendations.
   C. Every statement that is a conclusion should grow out of facts given elsewhere in the report.
   D. Conclusions and recommendations should always conclude the report because they depend on its contents.

2. Assume you are preparing a systematic analysis of our agency's pest control program and its effect on eliminating rodent infestation of premises in a specific region. To omit from your report important facts which you originally received from the person to whom you are recording is GENERALLY considered to be
   A. *desirable*; anyone who is likely to read the report can consult his files for extra information
   B. *undesirable*; the report should include major facts that are obtained as a result of your efforts
   C. *desirable*; the person you are reporting to does not pass the report on to others who lack his own familiarity with the subject
   D. *undesirable*; the report should include all of the facts that are obtained as a result of your efforts

3. Of all the non-verbal devices used in report writing, tables are used most frequently to enable a reader to compare statistical information more easily. Hence, it is important that an analyst know when to use tables.
   Which one of the following statements that relate to tables is generally considered to be LEAST valid?
   A. A table from an outside source must be acknowledged by the report writer.
   B. A table should be placed far in advance of the point where it is referred to or discussed in the report.
   C. The notes applying to a table are placed at the bottom of the table, rather than at the bottom of the page on which the table is found.
   D. A table should indicate the major factors that effect the data it contains.

4. Assume that an analyst writes reports which contain more detail than might be needed to serve their purpose. Such a practice is GENERALLY considered to be
   A. *desirable*; this additional detail permits maximized machine utilization
   B. *undesirable*; if specifications of reports are defined when they are first set up, loss of flexibility will follow

C. *desirable*; everything ought to be recorded so it will be there if it is ever needed
D. *undesirable*; recipients of these reports are likely to discredit them entirely

Questions 5-6.

DIRECTIONS: Questions 5 and 6 consist of sentences lettered A, B, C, and D. For each question, choose the sentence which is stylistically and grammatically MOST appropriate for a management report.

5. A. For too long, the citizen has been forced to rely for his productivity information on the whims, impressions, and uninformed opinion of public spokesmen.
   B. For too long, the citizen has been forced to base his information about productivity on the whims, impressions and uninformed opinion of public spokesmen.
   C. The citizen has been forced do base his information about productivity on the whims, impressions and uninformed opinion of public spokesmen for too long.
   D. The citizen has been forced for too long to rely for his productivity information on the whims, impressions and uninformed opinion of public spokesmen.

6. A. More competition means lower costs to the city, thereby helping to compensate for inflation.
   B. More competition, helping to compensate for inflation, means lower costs to the city.
   C. Inflation may be compensated for by more competition, which will reduce the city's costs.
   D. The costs to the city will be lessened by more competition, helping to compensate for inflation.

Questions 7-11.

DIRECTIONS: In Questions 7 through 11, choose the sentence which is BEST from the point of view of English usage suitable for a business letter or report.

7. A. It is the opinion of the Commissioners that programs which include the construction of cut-rate municipal garages in the central business district is inadvisable.
   B. Having reviewed the material submitted, the program for putting up cut-rate garages in the central business district seemed likely to cause traffic congestion.
   C. The Commissioners believe that putting up cut-rate municipal garages in the central business district is inadvisable.
   D. Making an effort to facilitate the cleaning of streets in the central business district, the building of cut-rate municipal garages presents the problem that it would encourage more motorists to come into the central city.

8. A. This letter, together with the reports, are to be sent to the principal.
    B. The reports, together with this letter, is to be sent to the principal.
    C. The reports and this letter is to be sent to the principal.
    D. This letter, together with the reports, is to be sent to the principal.

9. A. Each employee has to decide for themselves whether to take the examination.
    B. Each of the employees has to decide or himself whether to take the examination.
    C. Each of the employees has to decide for themselves whether to take the examination.
    D. Each of the employees have to decide for himself whether to take the examination.

10. A. The reason a new schedule is being prepared is that there has been a change in priorities.
    B. Because there has been a change in priorities is the reason why a new schedule is being made up.
    C. The reason why a new schedule is being made up is because there been a change in priorities.
    D. Because of a change in priorities is the reason why a new schedule is being prepared.

11. A. The changes in procedure had an unfavorable affect upon the output of the unit.
    B. The increased output of the unit was largely due to the affect of the procedural changes.
    C. The changes in procedure had the effect of increasing the output of the unit.
    D. The increased output of the unit from the procedural changes were the effect.

Questions 12-19.

DIRECTIONS: Questions 12 through 19 each consist of four sentences. Choose the one sentence in each set of four that would be BEST for a formal letter or report. Consider grammar and appropriate usage.

12. A. These statements can be depended on, for their truth has been guaranteed by reliable employees.
    B. Reliable city employees guarantee the facts with regards to the truth of these statements.
    C. Most all these statements have been supported by city employees who are reliable and can be depended upon.
    D. The city employees which have guaranteed these statements are reliable.

13. A. I believe the letter was addressed to either my associate or I.
    B. If properly addressed, the letter will reach my associate and I.
    C. My associate's name, as well as mine, was on the letter.
    D. The letter had been addressed to myself and my associate.

14. A. The secretary would have corrected the errors if she knew that the supervisor would see the report. 14.____
     B. The supervisor reprimanded the secretary, whom she believed had made careless errors.
     C. Many errors were found in the report which she typed and could not disregard.
     D. The errors in the typed report were so numerous that they could hardly be overlooked.

15. A. His consultant was as pleased as he with the success of the project. 15.____
     B. The success of the project pleased both his consultant and he.
     C. He and also his consultant was pleased with the success of the project.
     D. Both his consultant and he was pleased with the success of the project.

16. A. Since the letter did not contain the needed information, he could not use it. 16.____
     B. Being that the letter lacked the needed information, he could not use it.
     C. Since the letter lacked the needed information, it was of no use to him.
     D. This letter was useless to him because there was no needed information in it.

17. A. Scarcely had the real estate tax increase been declared than the notices were sent out. 17.____
     B. They had no sooner declared the real estate tax increases when they sent the notices to the owners.
     C. The city had hardly declared the real estate tax increase till the notices were prepared for mailing.
     D. No sooner had the real estate tax increase been declared than the notices were sent out

18. A. Though deeply effected by the setback, the advice given by the admissions office began to seem more reasonable. 18.____
     B. Although he was deeply effected by the setback, the advice given by the admissions office began to seem more reasonable.
     C. Though the setback had affected him deeply, the advise given by the admissions office began to see more reasonable.
     D. Although he was deeply affected by the setback, the advice given by the admissions office began to seem more reasonable.

19. A. Returning to the administration building after attendance at a meeting, the door was locked despite an agreement that it would be left open. 19.____
     B. When he returned to the administration building after attending a meeting, he found the door locked, despite an agreement that it would be left open.
     C. After attending a meeting, the door to the administration building was locked, despite an agreement that it would be left open.
     D. When he returned to the administration building after attendance at a meeting, he found the door locked, despite an agreement that it would be left open.

5 (#3)

20. A. A formal business report may consist of many parts, including the following:
    1. Table of Contents
    2. List of references
    3. Preface
    4. Index
    5. List of Tables
    6. Conclusions or recommendations

    Of the following, in setting up a formal report, the PROPER order of the six parts listed is:
    A. 1, 3, 6, 5, 2, 4
    B. 4, 3, 2, 5, 6 1
    C. 3, 1, 5, 6, 2, 4
    D. 2, 5, 3, 1, 4, 6

21. Suppose you are writing a report on an interview you have just completed with a particularly hostile applicant for public assistance.
    Which of the following BEST describes what you should include in this report?
    A. What you think caused the applicant's hostile attitude during the interview
    B. Specific examples of the applicant's hostile remarks and behavior
    C. The relevant information uncovered during the interview
    D. A recommendation that the applicant's request be denied because of his hostility.

22. When including recommendations in a report to your supervisor, which of the following is MOST important for you to do?
    A. Provide several alternative courses of action for each recommendation.
    B. First present the supporting evidence, then the recommendations.
    C. First present the recommendations, then the supporting evidence.
    D. Make sure the recommendations arise logically out of the information in the report.

23. It is often necessary that the writer of a report present facts and sufficient arguments to gain acceptance of the points, conclusions, or recommendations set forth in the report.
    Of the following, the LEAST advisable step to take in organizing a report, when such argumentation is the important factor, is a(n)
    A. elaborate expression of personal belief
    B. businesslike discussion of the problem as a whole
    C, orderly arrangement of convincing data
    D. reasonable explanation of the primary issues

24. Assume that a clerk is asked to prepare a special report which he has not prepared before. He decides to make a written outline of the report before writing it in full. This decision by the clerk is
    A. *good*, mainly because it helps the writer to organize his thoughts and decide what will go into the report
    B. *good*, mainly because it clearly shows the number of topics, number of '

C. *poor*, mainly because it wastes the time of the writer since he will have to write the full report anyway.
D. *poor*, mainly because it confines the writer to those areas listed in the outline

25. Assume that a clerk in the water resources central shop is asked to prepare an important report, giving the location and condition of various fire hydrants in the city. One of the hydrants in question is broken and is spewing rusty water in the street, creating a flooded condition in the area. The clerk reports that the hydrant is broken but does not report the escaping water or the flood.
Of the following, the BEST evaluation of the clerk's decision about what to report is that it is basically
   A. *correct*; chiefly because a lengthy report would contain irrelevant information
   B. *correct*; chiefly because a more detailed description of a hydrant should be made by a fireman, not a clerk
   C. *incorrect*; chiefly because the clerk's assignment was to describe the condition of the hydrant and he should give a full explanation
   D. *incorrect*; chiefly because the clerk should include as much information as possible in his report whether or not it is relevant

25.____

KEY (CORRECT ANSWERS)

1.	C		11.	C
2.	B		12.	A
3.	B		13.	C
4.	D		14.	D
5.	B		15.	A
6.	A		16.	C
7.	C		17.	D
8.	D		18.	D
9.	B		19.	B
10.	A		20.	C

21.	C
22.	D
23.	A
24.	A
25.	C

PREPARING WRITTEN MATERIALS
EXAMINATION SECTION
TEST 1

DIRECTIONS: Each question consists of a sentence which may be classified appropriately under one of the following four categories:
- A. Incorrect because of faulty grammar or sentence structure.
- B. Incorrect because of faulty punctuation.
- C. Incorrect because of faulty spelling or capitalization.
- D. Correct

Examine each sentence carefully. Then, in the space at the right, print the capital letter preceding the option which is the BEST of the four suggested above. All incorrect sentences contain only one type of error. Consider a sentence correct if it contains none of the types of errors mentioned, although there may be other correct ways of expressing the same thought.

1. The fire apparently started in the storeroom, which is usually locked.   1.____

2. On approaching the victim two bruises were noticed by this officer.   2.____

3. The officer, who was there examined the report with great care.   3.____

4. Each employee in the office had a separate desk.   4.____

5. The suggested procedure is similar to the one now in use.   5.____

6. No one was more pleased with the new procedure than the chauffeur.   6.____

7. He tried to pursuade her to change the procedure.   7.____

8. The total of the expenses charged to petty cash were high.   8.____

9. An understanding between him and I was finally reached.   9.____

10. It was at the supervisor's request that the clerk agreed to postpone his vacation.   10.____

11. We do not believe that it is necessary for both he and the clerk to attend the conference.   11.____

12. All employees, who display perseverance, will be given adequate recognition.   12.____

13. He regrets that some of us employees are dissatisfied with our new assignments.   13.____

14. "Do you think that the raise was merited," asked the supervisor? 14.____

15. The new manual of procedure is a valuable supplament to our rules and regulation. 15.____

16. The typist admitted that she had attempted to pursuade the other employees to assist her in her work. 16.____

17. The supervisor asked that all amendments to the regulations be handled by you and I. 17.____

18. They told both he and I that the prisoner had escaped. 18.____

19. Any superior officer, who, disregards the just complaints of his subordinates, is remiss in the performance of his duty. 19.____

20. Only those members of the national organization who resided in the Middle west attended the conference in Chicago. 20.____

21. We told him to give the investigation assignment to whoever was available. 21.____

22. Please do not disappoint and embarass us by not appearing in court. 22.____

23. Despite the efforts of the Supervising mechanic, the elevator could not be started. 23.____

24. The U.S. Weather Bureau, weather record for the accident date was checked. 24.____

KEY (CORRECT ANSWERS)

1.	D	11.	A
2.	A	12.	B
3.	B	13.	D
4.	D	14.	B
5.	D	15.	C
6.	D	16.	C
7.	C	17.	A
8.	A	18.	A
9.	A	19.	B
10.	D	20.	C

21. D
22. C
23. C
24. B

TEST 2

DIRECTIONS: Each question consists of a sentence. Some of the sentences contain errors in English grammar or usage, punctuation, spelling, or capitalization. A sentence does not contain an error simply because it could be written in a different manner. Choose answer:
- A. If the sentence contains an error in English grammar or usage.
- B. if the sentence contains an error in punctuation.
- C. If the sentence contains an error in spelling or capitalization
- D. If the sentence does not contain any errors.

1. The severity of the sentence prescribed by contemporary statutes—including both the former and the revised New York Penal Laws—do not depend on what crime was intended by the offender. 1.____

2. It is generally recognized that two defects in the early law of attempt played a part in the birth of burglary: (1) immunity from prosecution for conduct short of the last act before completion of the crime, and (2) the relatively minor penalty imposed for an attempt (it being a common law misdemeanor) vis-à-vis the completed offense. 2.____

3. The first sentence of the statute is applicable to employees who enter their place of employment, invited guests, and all other persons who have an express or implied license or privilege to enter the premises. 3.____

4. Contemporary criminal codes in the United States generally divide burglary into various degrees, differentiating the categories according to place, time and other attendent circumstances. 4.____

5. The assignment was completed in record time but the payroll for it has not yet been prepaid. 5.____

6. The operator, on the other hand, is willing to learn me how to use the mimeograph. 6.____

7. She is the prettiest of the three sisters. 7.____

8. She doesn't know; if the mail has arrived. 8.____

9. The doorknob of the office door is broke. 9.____

10. Although the department's supply of scratch pads and stationery have diminished considerably, the allotment for our division has not been reduced. 10.____

11. You have not told us whom you wish to designate as your secretary. 11.____

12. Upon reading the minutes of the last meeting, the new proposal was taken up for consideration. 12.____

13. Before beginning the discussion, we locked the door as a precautionery measure.   13._____

14. The supervisor remarked, "Only those clerks, who perform routine work, are permitted to take a rest period."   14._____

15. Not only will this duplicating machine make accurate copies, but it will also produce a quantity of work equal to fifteen transcribing typists.   15._____

16. "Mr. Jones," said the supervisor, "we regret our inability to grant you an extention of your leave of absence."   16._____

17. Although the employees find the work monotonous and fatigueing, they rarely complain.   17._____

18. We completed the tabulation of the receipts on time despite the fact that Miss Smith our fastest operator was absent for over a week.   18._____

19. The reaction of the employees who attended the meeting, as well as the reaction of those who did not attend, indicates clearly that the schedule is satisfactory to everyone concerned.   19._____

20. Of the two employees, the one in our office is the most efficient.   20._____

21. No one can apply or even understand, the new rules and regulations.   21._____

22. A large amount of supplies were stored in the empty office.   22._____

23. If an employee is occassionally asked to work overtime, he should do so willingly.   23._____

24. It is true that the new procedures are difficult to use but, we are certain that you will learn them quickly.   24._____

25. The office manager said that he did not know who would be given a large allotment under the new plan.   25._____

KEY (CORRECT ANSWERS)

1.	A	11.	D
2.	D	12.	A
3.	D	13.	C
4.	C	14.	B
5.	C	15.	A
6.	A	16.	C
7.	D	17.	C
8.	B	18.	B
9.	A	19.	D
10.	A	20.	A

21. B
22. A
23. C
24. B
25. D

TEST 3

DIRECTIONS: Each of the following sentences may be classified MOST appropriately under one of the following categories:
   A. Faulty because of incorrect grammar
   B. Faulty because of incorrect punctuation
   C. Faulty because of incorrect capitalization
   D. Correct

Examine each sentence carefully. Then, in the space at the right, print the capital letter preceding the option which is the BEST of the four suggested above. All incorrect sentence contain but one type of error. Consider a sentence correct if it contains none of the types of errors mentioned, even though there may be other correct ways of expressing the same thought.

1. The desk, as well as the chairs, were moved out of the office.   1.____

2. The clerk whose production was greatest for the month won a day's vacation as first prize.   2.____

3. Upon entering the room, the employees were found hard at work at their desks.   3.____

4. John Smith our new employee always arrives at work on time.   4.____

5. Punish whoever is guilty of stealing the money.   5.____

6. Intelligent and persistent effort lead to success no matter what the job may be.   6.____

7. The secretary asked, "can you call again at three o'clock?"   7.____

8. He told us, that if the report was not accepted at the next meeting, it would have to be rewritten.   8.____

9. He would not have sent the letter if he had known that it would cause so much excitement.   9.____

10. We all looked forward to him coming to visit us.   10.____

11. If you find that you are unable to complete the assignment please notify me as soon as possible.   11.____

12. Every girl in the office went home on time but me; there was still some work for me to finish.   12.____

13. He wanted to know who the letter was addressed to, Mr. Brown or Mr. Smith.   13.____

14. "Mr. Jones, he said, please answer this letter as soon as possible."   14.____

135

15. The new clerk had an unusual accent inasmuch as he was born and educated in the south.   15._____

16. Although he is younger than her, he earns a higher salary.   16._____

17. Neither of the two administrators are going to attend the conference being held in Washington, D.C.   17._____

18. Since Miss Smith and Miss Jones have more experience than us, they have been given more responsible duties.   18._____

19. Mr. Shaw the supervisor of the stock room maintains an inventory of stationery and office supplies.   19._____

20. Inasmuch as this matter affects both you and I, we should take joint action.   20._____

21. Who do you think will be able to perform this highly technical work?   21._____

22. Of the two employees, John is considered the most competent.   22._____

23. He is not coming home on tuesday; we expect him next week.   23._____

24. Stenographers, as well as typists must be able to type rapidly and accurately.   24._____

25. Having been placed in the safe we were sure that the money would not be stolen.   25._____

KEY (CORRECT ANSWERS)

1.	A		11.	B
2.	D		12.	D
3.	A		13.	A
4.	B		14.	B
5.	D		15.	C
6.	A		16.	A
7.	C		17.	A
8.	B		18.	A
9.	D		19.	B
10.	A		20.	A

21. D
22. A
23. C
24. B
25. A

TEST 4

DIRECTIONS: Each of the following sentences consist of four sentences lettered A, B, C, and D. One of the sentences in each group contains an error in grammar or punctuation. Indicate the INCORRECT sentence in each group. *PRINT THE LETTER OF THE CORRECT ANSWER IN THE SPACE AT THE RIGHT.*

1. A. Give the message to whoever is on duty.
    B. The teacher who's pupil won first prize presented the award.
    C. Between you and me, I don't expect the program to succeed.
    D. His running to catch the bus caused the accident.
    1.____

2. A. The process, which was patented only last year is already obsolete.
    B. His interest in science (which continues to the present) led him to convert his basement into a laboratory.
    C. He described the book as "verbose, repetitious, and bombastic".
    D. Our new director will need to possess three qualities: vision, patience, and fortitude.
    2.____

3. A. The length of ladder trucks varies considerably.
    B. The probationary fireman reported to the officer to who he was assigned.
    C. The lecturer emphasized the need for we firemen to be punctual.
    D. Neither the officers nor the members of the company knew about the new procedure.
    3.____

4. A. Ham and eggs is the specialty of the house.
    B. He is one of the students who are on probation.
    C. Do you think that either one of us have a chance to be nominated for president of the class?
    D. I assume that either he was to be in charge or you were.
    4.____

5. A. Its a long road that has no turn.
    B. To run is more tiring than to walk.
    C. We have been assigned three new reports: namely, the statistical summary, the narrative summary, and the budgetary summary.
    D. Had the first payment been made in January, the second would be due in April.
    5.____

6. A. Each employer has his own responsibilities.
    B. If a person speaks correctly, they make a good impression.
    C. Every one of the operators has had her vacation.
    D. Has anybody filed his report?
    6.____

7. A. The manager, with all his salesmen, was obliged to go.
    B. Who besides them is to sign the agreement?
    C. One report without the others is incomplete.
    D. Several clerks, as well as the proprietor, was injured.
    7.____

8.
- A. A suspension of these activities is expected.
- B. The machine is economical because first cost and upkeep are low.
- C. A knowledge of stenography and filing are required for this position.
- D. The condition in which the goods were received shows that the packing was not done properly.

8.____

9.
- A. There seems to be a great many reasons for disagreement.
- B. It does not seem possible that they could have failed.
- C. Have there always been too few applicants for these positions?
- D. There is no excuse for these errors.

9.____

10.
- A. We shall be pleased to answer your question.
- B. Shall we plan the meeting for Saturday?
- C. I will call you promptly at seven.
- D. Can I borrow your book after you have read it?

10.____

11.
- A. You are as capable as I.
- B. Everyone is willing to sign but him and me.
- C. As for he and his assistant, I cannot praise them too highly.
- D. Between you and me, I think he will be dismissed.

11.____

12.
- A. Our competitors bid above us last week.
- B. The survey which was began last year has not yet been completed.
- C. The operators had shown that they understood their instructions.
- D. We have never ridden over worse roads.

12.____

13.
- A. Who did they say was responsible?
- B. Whom did you suspect?
- C. Who do you suppose it was?
- D. Whom do you mean?

13.____

14.
- A. Of the two propositions, this is the worse.
- B. Which report do you consider the best—the one in January or the one in July?
- C. I believe this is the most practicable of the many plans submitted.
- D. He is the youngest employee in the organization.

14.____

15.
- A. The firm had but three orders last week.
- B. That doesn't really seem possible.
- C. After twenty years scarcely none of the old business remains.
- D. Has he done nothing about it?

15.____

KEY (CORRECT ANSWERS)

1.	B	6.	B	11.	C
2.	A	7.	D	12.	B
3.	C	8.	C	13.	A
4.	C	9.	A	14.	B
5.	A	10.	D	15.	C

PREPARING WRITTEN MATERIAL

PARAGRAPH REARRANGEMENT
COMMENTARY

The sentences that follow are in scrambled order. You are to rearrange them in proper order and indicate the letter choice containing the correct answer at the space at the right.

Each group of sentences in this section is actually a paragraph presented in scrambled order. Each sentence in the group has a place in that paragraph; no sentence is to be left out. You are to read each group of sentences and decide upon the best order in which to put the sentences so as to form a well-organized paragraph.

The questions in this section measure the ability to solve a problem when all the facts relevant to its solution are not given.

More specifically, certain positions of responsibility and authority require the employee to discover connection between events sometimes, apparently, unrelated. In order to do this, the employee will find it necessary to correctly infer that unspecified events have probably occurred or are likely to occur. This ability becomes especially important when action must be taken on incomplete information.

Accordingly, these questions require competitors to choose among several suggested alternatives, each of which presents a different sequential arrangement of the events. Competitors must choose the MOST logical of the suggested sequences.

In order to do so, they may be required to draw on general knowledge to infer missing concepts or events that are essential to sequencing the given events. Competitors should be careful to infer only what is essential to the sequence. The plausibility of the wrong alternatives will always require the inclusion of unlikely events or of additional chains of events which are NOT essential to sequencing the given events.

It's very important to remember that you are looking for the best of the four possible choices, and that the best choice of all may not even be one of the answers you're given to choose from.

There is no one right way to solve these problems. Many people have found it helpful to first write out the order of the sentences, as they would have arranged them, on their scrap paper before looking at the possible answers. If their optimum answer is there, this can save them some time. If it isn't, this method can still give insight into solving the problem. Others find it most helpful to just go through each of the possible choices, contrasting each as they go along. You should use whatever method feels comfortable and works for you.

While most of these types of questions are not that difficult, we've added a higher percentage of the difficult type, just to give you more practice. Usually there are only one or two questions on this section that contain such subtle distinctions that you're unable to answer confidently. And you then may find yourself stuck deciding between two possible choices, neither of which you're sure about.

EXAMINATION SECTION

TEST 1

DIRECTIONS: Each question consists of several sentences which can be arranged in a logical sequence. For each question, select the choice which places the numbered sentences in the MOST logical sequence. *PRINT THE LETTER OF THE CORRECT ANSWER IN THE SPACE AT THE RIGHT.*

1.
   I. A body was found in the woods.
   II. A man proclaimed innocence.
   III. The owner of a gun was located.
   IV. A gun was traced.
   V. The owner of a gun was questioned.
   The CORRECT answer is:
   A. IV, III, V, II, I
   B. II, I, IV, III, V
   C. I, IV, III, V, II
   D. I, III, V, II, IV
   E. I, II, IV, III, V

   1.____

2.
   I. A man is in a hunting accident.
   II. A man fell down a flight of steps.
   III. A man lost his vision in one eye,
   IV. A man broke his leg.
   V. A man had to walk with a cane.
   The CORRECT answer is:
   A. II, IV, V, I, III
   B. IV, V, I, III, II
   C. III, I, IV, V, II
   D. I, III, V, II, IV
   E. I, III, II, IV, V

   2.____

3.
   I. A man is offered a new job.
   II. A woman is offered a new job.
   III. A man works as a waiter.
   IV. A woman works as a waitress.
   V. A woman gives notice.
   The CORRECT answer is:
   A. IV, II, V, III, I
   B. IV, II, V, I, III
   C. II, IV, V, III, I
   D. III, I, IV, II, V
   E. IV, III, II, V, I

   3.____

4.
   I. A train let the station late.
   II. A man was late for work.
   III. A man lost his job.
   IV. Many people complained because the train was late.
   V. There was a traffic jam.
   The CORRECT answer is:
   A. V, II, I, IV, III
   B. V, I, IV, II, III
   C. V, I, II, IV, III
   D. I, V, IV, II, III
   E. II, I, IV, V, III

   4.____

5. I. The burden of proof as to each issue is determined before trial and remains upon the same party throughout the trial.
    II. The jury is at liberty to believe one witness' testimony as against a number of contradictory witnesses.
    III. In a civil case, the party bearing the burden of proof is required to prove his contention by a fair preponderance of the evidence.
    IV. However, it must be noted that a fair preponderance of evidence does not necessarily mean a greater number of witnesses.
    V. The burden of proof is the burden which rests upon one of the parties to an action to persuade the trier of the facts, generally the jury, that a proposition he asserts is true.
    VI. If the evidence is equally balanced, or if it leaves the jury in such doubt as to be unable to decide the controversy either way, judgment must be given against the party upon whom the burden of proof rests.
    The CORRECT answer is:
    A. III, II, V, IV, I, VI   B. I, II, VI, V, III, IV   C. III, IV, V, I, II, VI
    D. V, I, III, VI, IV, II   E. I, V, III, VI, IV, II

5.____

6. I. If a parent is without assets and is unemployed, he cannot be convicted of the crime of non-support of a child.
    II. The term *sufficient ability* has been held to mean sufficient financial ability.
    III. It does not matter if his unemployment is by choice or unavoidable circumstances.
    IV. If he fails to take any steps at all, he may be liable to prosecution for endangering the welfare of a child.
    V. Under the penal law, a parent is responsible for the support of his minor child only if the parent is of *sufficient ability*.
    VI. An indigent parent may meet his obligation by borrowing money or by seeking aid under the provisions of the Social Welfare Law.
    The CORRECT answer is:
    A. VI, I, V, III, II, IV   B. I, III, V, II, IV, VI   C. V, II, I, III, VI, IV
    D. I, VI, IV, V, II, III   E. II, V, I, III, VI, IV

6.____

7. I. Consider, for example, the case of a rabble rouser who urges a group of twenty people to go out and break the windows of a nearby factory.
    II. Therefore, the law fills the indicated gap with the crime of *inciting to riot*.
    III. A person is considered guilty of inciting to riot when he urges ten or more persons to engage in tumultuous and violent conduct of a kind likely to create public alarm.
    IV. However, if he has not obtained the cooperation of at least four people, he cannot be charged with unlawful assembly.
    V. The charge of inciting to riot was added to the law to cover types of conduct which cannot be classified as either the crime of *riot* or the crime of *unlawful assembly*.
    VI. If he acquires the acquiescence of at least four of them, he is guilty of unlawful assembly even if the project does not materialize.
    The CORRECT answer is:
    A. III, V, I, VI, IV, II   B. V, I, IV, VI, II, III   C. III, IV, I, V, II, VI
    D. V, I, IV, VI, III, II   E. V, III, I, VI, IV, II

7.____

8. I. If, however, the rebuttal evidence presents an issue of credibility, it is for the jury to determine whether the presumption has, in fact, been destroyed.
    II. Once sufficient evidence to the contrary is introduced, the presumption disappears from the trial.
    III. The effect of a presumption is to place the burden upon the adversary to come forward with evidence to rebut the presumption.
    IV. When a presumption is overcome and ceases to exist in the case, the fact or facts which gave rise to the presumption still remain.
    V. Whether a presumption has been overcome is ordinarily a question for the court.
    VI. Such information may furnish a basis for a logical inference.
    The CORRECT answer is:
    A. IV, VI, II, V, I, III   B. III, II, V, I, IV, VI   C. V, III, VI, IV, II, I
    D. V, IV, I, II, VI, III   E. II, III, V, I, IV, VI

    8.____

9. I. An executive may answer a letter by writing his reply on the face of the letter itself instead of having a return letter typed.
    II. This procedure is efficient because it saves the executive's time, the typist's time, and saves office file space.
    III. Copying machines are used in small offices as well as large offices to save time and money in making brief replies to business letters.
    IV. A copy is made on a copying machine to go into the company files, while the original is mailed back to the sender.
    The CORRECT answer is:
    A. I, II, IV, III   B. I, IV, II, III   C. III, I, IV, II   D. III, IV, II, I

    9.____

10. I. Most organizations favor one of the types but always include the others to a lesser degree.
    II. However, we can detect a definite trend toward greater use of symbolic control.
    III. We suggest that our local police agencies are today primarily utilizing material control.
    IV. Control can be classified into three types: physical, material, and symbolic.
    The CORRECT answer is:
    A. IV, II, III, I   B. II, I, IV, III   C. III, IV, II, I   D. IV, I, III, II

    10.____

11. I. Project residents had first claim to this use, followed by surrounding neighborhood children.
    II. By contrast, recreation space within the project's interior was found to be used more often by both groups.
    III. Studies of the use of project grounds in many cities showed grounds left open for public use were neglected and unused, both by residents and by members of the surrounding community.
    IV. Project residents had clearly laid claim to the play spaces, setting up and enforcing unwritten rules for use.
    V. Each group, by experience, found their activities easily disrupted by other groups, and their claim to the use of space for recreation difficult to enforce.

    11.____

The CORRECT answer is:
A. IV, V, I, II, III
B. V, II, IV, III, I
C. I, IV, III, II, V
D. III, V, II, IV, I

12. I. They do not consider the problems correctable within the existing subsidy formula and social policy of accepting all eligible applicants regardless of social behavior.
    II. A recent survey, however, indicated that tenants believe these problems correctable by local housing authorities and management within the existing financial formula.
    III. Many of the problems and complaints concerning public housing management and design have created resentment between the tenant and the landlord.
    IV. This same survey indicated that administrators and managers do not agree with the tenants.
    The CORRECT answer is:
    A. II, I, III, IV   B. I, III, IV, II   C. III, II, IV, I   D. IV, II, I, III

13. I. In single-family residences, there is usually enough distance between tenants to prevent occupants from annoying one another.
    II. For example, a certain small percentage of tenant families has one or more members addicted to alcohol.
    III. While managers believe in the right of individuals to live as they choose, the manager becomes concerned when the pattern of living jeopardizes others' rights.
    IV. Still others turn night into day, staging lusty entertainments which carry on into the hours when most tenants are trying to sleep.
    V. In apartment buildings, however, tenants live so closely together that any misbehavior can result in unpleasant living conditions.
    VI. Other families engage in violent argument.
    The CORRECT answer is:
    A. III, II, V, IV, VI, I
    B. I, V, II, VI, IV, III
    C. II, V, IV, I, III, VI
    D. IV, II, V, VI, III, I

14. I. Congress made the commitment explicit in the Housing Act of 194, establishing as a national goal the realization of a *decent home and suitable environment for every American family*.
    II. The result has been that the goal of decent home and suitable environment is still as far distant as ever for the disadvantaged urban family.
    III. In spite of this action by Congress, federal housing programs have continued to be fragmented and grossly underfunded.
    IV. The passage of the National Housing Act signaled a few federal commitment to provide housing for the nation's citizens.
    The CORRECT answer is:
    A. I, IV, III, II   B. IV, I, III, II   C. IV, I, II, III   D. II, IV, I, III

15.
   I. The greater expense does not necessarily involve *exploitation*, but it is often perceived as exploitative and unfair by those who are aware of the price differences involved, but unaware of operating costs.
   II. Ghetto residents believe they are *exploited* by local merchants, and evidence substantiates some of these beliefs.
   III. However, stores in low-income areas were more likely to be small independents, which could not achieve the economies available to supermarket chains and were, therefore, more likely to charge higher prices, and the customers were more likely to buy smaller-sized packages which are more expensive per unit of measure.
   IV. A study conducted in one city showed that distinctly higher prices were charged for goods sold in ghetto stores in other areas.

   The CORRECT answer is:
   A. IV, II, I, III   B. IV, I, III, II   C. II, IV, III, I   D. II, III, IV, I

15._____

KEY (CORRECT ANSWERS)

1.	C	6.	C	11.	D
2.	E	7.	A	12.	C
3.	B	8.	B	13.	B
4.	B	9.	C	14.	B
5.	D	10.	D	15.	C